Traverse Theatre Company
in association with
National Theatre of Scotland

GUT

Frances Poet

First produced and performed at the Traverse Theatre, Scotland,
on 24 April 2018.

Commissioned by National Theatre of Scotland.
Part of National Theatre of Scotland's new writing initiative
with the Tron Theatre and the Traverse Theatre.

Company List

Cast
THE STRANGER	George Anton
RORY	Peter Collins
MORVEN	Lorraine McIntosh
MADDY	Kirsty Stuart

Creative Team
Writer	Frances Poet
Director	Zinnie Harris
Designer	Fred Meller
Lighting Designer	Kai Fischer
Composer & Sound Designer	Michael John McCarthy
Assistant Director University Placement	Isla Cowan

Production Team
Production Manager	Kevin McCallum
Chief Electrician	Renny Robertson
Deputy Electrician	Claire Elliot
Head of Stage	Gary Staerck
Lighting & Sound Technician	Tom Saunders
Company Stage Manager	Gemma Turner
Deputy Stage Manager	Gillian Richards
Assistant Stage Manager	Shellie Barrowcliffe
Costume Supervisor	Sophie Ferguson

Company Biographies

George Anton (The Stranger)
George trained at the Drama Centre, London.

Theatre credits include: *Oresteia: This Restless House* (Citizens Theatre/ Edinburgh International Festival); *The Duchess of Malfi* (Cheek By Jowl); *Life is a Dream* (Edinburgh International Festival/BAM); *Hamlet* (Edinburgh International Festival/Birmingham Repertory Theatre); *Paul Bright's Confessions of a Justified Sinner* (Edinburgh International Festival/Untitled Projects/ National Theatre of Scotland); *Titus Andronicus* (Dundee Rep).

Television credits include: *Marcella, Law & Order: UK, The Loch* (ITV).

Film credits include: *Calibre; Churchill; The Sweeney; K-19: The Widowmaker.*

Peter Collins (Rory)
Film and television credits include: *Outlander* (Starz); *The Secret Agent* (World Productions); *Eve* (Leopard Productions/CBBC); *Grease Monkeys, Casualty* (BBC); *Mile High* (Hewland International); *Peak Practice* (ITV); *The Hunt* (Carlton); and *Always and Everyone* (Granada).

Theatre credits include: *Richard III* (Perth Theatre); *Oresteia: This Restless House* (Citizens Theatre/Edinburgh International Festival); *Cinderella, Hansel and Gretel* (Citizens Theatre);*The Story of the Little Gentleman, White, The Ballad of Pondlife McGurk* (Catherine Wheels); *Tin Forest* (National Theatre of Scotland); *Horizontal Collaboration* (Fire Exit); *Much Ado About Nothing, The Taming of the Shrew* (Royal Exchange Theatre); *Hamlet: First Cut* (Red Shift); *How the Other Half Loves* (Bolton Octagon);*Ticket To Write/Northern Exposure* (Paines Plough); *The Tempest* (Compass Theatre Company); *Caucasian Chalk Circle* (National Theatre); *Temptations and Betrayals* (Bristol New Vic); *Grimm Tales* (Leicester Haymarket); *Macbeth, Thebans, Medea, King Lear, Julius Caesar, Hamlet, Romeo and Juliet* (Theatre Babel); *Macbeth, Julius Caesar, Maggie May, Marat/Sade* (National Youth Theatre).

Kai Fischer (Lighting Designer)
Lighting design credits for the Traverse Theatre include: *How to Disappear, I Was a Beautiful Day, Gorgeous Avatar, The Pearlfisher* and *One Day All This Will Come to Nothing.* Kai recently designed set and costume for the Traverse Theatre Company production of *Tracks of the Winter Bear.*

Lighting designs for other companies include: *Tabula Rasa, Tomorrow* (Vanishing Point); *Cockpit, Charlie Sonata, Irma Vep, Blood and Ice, Woyzeck* (Royal Lyceum Theatre Edinburgh); *Wallace* (The Arches); *Great Expectations* (Beckman Unicorn/West End); *One Million Tiny Plays About Britain, Othello, Museum of Dreams, The Dance of Death, Endgame* (Citizens Theatre); *Medea's Children* (Lung Ha); *Eve, The Tin Forest, Riot of Spring, Pink Mist, Gobbo, Julie* (National Theatre of Scotland); *The Demon Barber, Phedre, Cinderella, Pinocchio* (Perth Theatre); *Brigadoon* (Royal Conservatoire of Scotland); *Oresteia* (SummerScape, New York); *4.48 Psychosis* (Sweetscar); *Macbeth* (Theatre Babel/Hong Kong Cultural Centre); *The Indian Wants The Bronx* (Young Vic).

Set and lighting design credits for other companies include: *Duke Bluebeard's Castle/The 8th Door, Ines de Castro* (Scottish Opera); *The Destroyed Room,*

The Beautiful Cosmos of Ivor Cutler, Wonderland, Saturday Night, Interiors
(Vanishing Point); *Fewer Emergencies, Heer Ranjha* (Ankur Productions);
Somersault, Allotment 3 and 4, Mancub, Little Otik, Home Caithness (National
Theatre of Scotland); *Grit* (Pachamama); *A Midsummer Night's Dream,
Wondrous Flitting* (Royal Lyceum Theatre Edinburgh); *Kind of Silence* (Solar
Bear); *Mister Holgado* (Unicorn Theatre); *One Night Stand* (Nick Underwood).

Own projects include: *Last Dream (On Earth)* (with National Theatre of
Scotland and Tron Theatre) and the performance and installation piece *Entartet*
(with Vanishing Point and CCA Glasgow).

Zinnie Harris (Director)

Zinnie Harris is a playwright and theatre director. Her plays include *Meet Me At
Dawn* (Traverse Theatre/Edinburgh International Festival); *Oresteia: This Restless
House* (Citizens Theatre/Edinburgh International Festival), winner of Best New
Play at the Critics' Awards for Theatre in Scotland 2016, and shortlisted for the
Susan Smith Blackburn Award; *How To Hold Your Breath* (Royal Court Theatre),
winner of the Berwin Lee Award 2015; *The Message* and *On The Watch*
(Tricycle Theatre); *The Wheel* (National Theatre of Scotland), joint winner of the
2011 Amnesty International Freedom of Expression Award and Fringe First
Award, shortlisted for the Susan Smith Blackburn Award; *The Panel* (Tricycle
Theatre); *The Garden, Fall* (Traverse Theatre); *Solstice* (Royal Shakespeare
Company); *Midwinter* (Royal Shakespeare Company), winner of an Arts
Foundation Fellowship Award for Playwriting, and shortlisted for the Susan Smith
Blackburn Award; *Nightingale and Chase* (Royal Court Theatre); and *Further
Than The Furthest Thing* (National Theatre/Tron Theatre), which was winner of
the Peggy Ramsay Playwriting Award, the John Whiting Award and Fringe First
Award as well as being specially commended by the Susan Smith Blackburn
Award, and shortlisted for the Evening Standard Most Promising Playwright; *By
Many Wounds* (Hampstead Theatre), shortlisted for the Allied Domecq Award
and the Meyer Whitworth Award. Adaptations include: *Rhinoceros* (Royal
Lyceum Theatre/Edinburgh International Festival); *A Doll's House* (Donmar
Warehouse); *Miss Julie* (National Theatre of Scotland).

As a theatre director she has directed productions for the Royal Shakespeare
Company, Traverse Theatre, Royal Lyceum Theatre Edinburgh, National Theatre
of Scotland, 7:84 and Tron Theatre. She has been Associate Director at the
Traverse Theatre since 2015 where she has directed a number of productions
including *Tracks of the Winter Bear* and *The Garden*. She won Best Director at
the Critics' Awards for Theatre in Scotland 2017, for her direction of Caryl
Churchill's *A Number* at the Royal Lyceum Theatre Edinburgh.

Michael John McCarthy (Composer & Sound Designer)
Michael John is a Cork-born, Glasgow-based composer, musician and sound designer.

Work for theatre includes: *How To Disappear, Grain In The Blood* (Traverse Theatre); *Trainspotting, The Gorbals Vampire, Rapunzel, Into That Darkness, Fever Dream: Southside* and *Sports Day* (Citizens Theatre); *Rocket Post, In Time O' Strife, Blabbermouth, The Tin Forest, The Day I Swapped My Dad For Two Goldfish, Truant, Dolls* (National Theatre of Scotland); *August: Osage County, George's Marvellous Medicine, The Cheviot, The Stag and The Black, Black Oil, The BFG* and *Steel Magnolias* (Dundee Rep Theatre); *Jimmy's Hall* (Abbey Theatre); *Futureproof* (Everyman Cork); *Glory on Earth, A Number, The Weir, Bondagers* (Royal Lyceum Theatre Edinburgh); *God of Carnage, The Lonesome West, Under Milk Wood* (Tron Theatre); *Light Boxes, Letters Home: England in a Pink Blouse, The Authorised Kate Bane* (Grid Iron); *Showtime from the Frontline, The Red Shed* (Mark Thomas/Lakin McCarthy); *Un Petit Molière, The Silent Treatment* (Lung Ha); *Bright Black, The Not-So-Fatal Death of Grandpa Fredo* (Vox Motus); *Ceilidh* (Theatre Gu Leòr); *J.R.R. Tolkien's Leaf By Niggle* (Puppet State Theatre); *The Interference* (Pepperdine); *Heads Up* (Kieran Hurley/Show & Tell); *A Gambler's Guide To Dying* (Gary McNair/Show & Tell); *Glory* (Janice Parker Projects); *The Winter's Tale* (People's Light and Theatre Company, Philadelphia).

Work for film includes: *Where You're Meant To Be* (Paul Fegan); *Hey Ronnie Reagan, Pitching Up* (Maurice O'Brien); *Spores* (Richard and Frances Poet).

He is lead artist on *Turntable*, a participatory arts project in association with Red Bridge.

Lorraine McIntosh (Morven)

Lorraine's first foray into professional acting was in 1998, in Ken Loach's award-winning film *My Name is Joe*. Prior to this, she concentrated on a successful musical career as vocalist with Deacon Blue, whose credits include two number one albums and seventeen top twenty singles. She continues to record and tour with the band, having released their most recent album *Believers* in September 2016, which entered the UK charts at number 12.

Theatre work includes: *Still Game* (Phil McIntyre Entertainment); *Beowulf, God of Carnage* (Tron Theatre); *Mum's The Word* (Robert C Kelly Productions); *Let the Right One In, Men Should Weep* and *Beautiful Burnout* (National Theatre of Scotland); and *Sixteen* (The Arches).

Television work includes: *Long Night at Blackstone* (Hopscotch Productions for BBC); *Scot Squad* (BBC); *Happy Holidays* (Effingee Productions); *West End Girls* (Solus Productions); *Hope Springs* (Shed Productions); *West Skerra Light* (Hopscotch Productions for BBC); *River City and Life Support* (BBC); and *Psychos* (Channel 4).

Film work includes: *Spores* (Hopscotch Productions); *Wilbur* (Dogma/Sigma Films) and *Aberdeen* (Freeway Films). Radio work includes: *In Search of Highland Mary,* and *Dan 50* (BBC Radio Scotland).

Fred Meller (Designer)

Notable theatre credits include: *Meet Me At Dawn* (Traverse Theatre/Edinburgh International Festival); *A Number* (Royal Lyceum Theatre Edinburgh), nominated for a 2017 Critics' Award for Theatre in Scotland; *Grain In The Blood* (Traverse Theatre/Tron Theatre); *Milk* (Traverse Theatre); *Swallow* (Traverse Theatre), winner of a Fringe First Award; *A Few Man Fridays* (Cardboard Citizens, The Riverside Studios); *Black Comedy* (The Watermill Theatre); *Woyzeck* (Cardboard Citizens/Southwark Playhouse); *Alaska* (Royal Court Theatre); *Timon of Athens* (Royal Shakespeare Company/Cardboard Citizens/The Complete Works Festival); *The Fever* (Young Vic); *Pericles* (Royal Shakespeare Company/Cardboard Citizens); *The Whizz Kid* (Almeida Theatre); *The Visitation of Mr Collioni* (Platform Four Theatre Company/Salisbury Playhouse); *Life With An Idiot* (The Gate Theatre/National Theatre); *Variety* (Grid Iron/Edinburgh International Festival); *Caledonian Road* (Almeida Theatre).

Fred is Course Leader for BA (Hons) Performance: Design and Practice at Central Saint Martins, University of the Arts, London. She co-convened the Scenography working group at TaPRA (Theatre and Performance Research Association), and is a Fellow of the HEA and The Arts Foundation.

Fred trained at The Royal Welsh College and received an Arts Council Designers Bursary. She works on productions that are representative of the devised, collaborative and new writing agendas that are her concerns, and continues to work collaboratively for new writing and site-specific projects, alongside established texts in traditional theatres.

Fred has exhibited at The Prague Quadrennial in 1999 and 2003, winning the Golden Triga, and was selected to exhibit at The World Stage Design in Toronto 2005, and in the National Society of British Theatre Designers Exhibitions. Her work is also part of the V&A Museum permanent collection. Other awards include The Jerwood Design Award and a Year of the Artist Award.

Frances Poet (Writer)

Frances is a Glasgow-based writer with sixteen years of experience working as a Dramaturg and Literary Manager in theatres across the UK. Frances has written for stage, TV and radio and has had short films screened at festivals nationally and internationally.

Her debut one-act play, *Faith Fall*, was presented at Orán Mòr, Glasgow and Bristol's Tobacco Factory in 2012. Since then she has completed a number of classic adaptations including *What Put The Blood* (Abbey Theatre); a free version of Racine's *Andromaque* (Peacock Stage, Abbey Theatre, Dublin and previously as *Andromaque* at Orán Mòr and The Byre Theatre, St Andrews); *The Macbeths,* adapted from Shakespeare's original with Dominic Hill (Circle Studio, Citizens Theatre); *Dance of Death*, after Strindberg (Circle Studio, Citizens Theatre); and *The Misanthrope,* after Molière (Orán Mòr).

Her play *Adam*, conceived and directed by Cora Bissett and produced by the National Theatre of Scotland at the Traverse Theatre, MacRobert Arts Centre and Citizens Theatre won Fringe First, Herald Angel and Scottish Arts Club awards at the 2017 Edinburgh Festival Fringe.

Frances is currently under commission to National Theatre of Scotland/Theatre Gu Leòr, Out of Joint and West Yorkshire Playhouse.

Kirsty Stuart (Maddy)

Kirsty trained at Drama Centre London.

Theatre credits include: *Oresteia: This Restless House* (Citizens Theatre/ Edinburgh International Festival); *Fever Dream: Southside* (Citizens Theatre); *Crude* and *Spring Awakening* (Grid Iron); *The Infamous Brothers Davenport* (Vox Motus/Royal Lyceum Theatre Edinburgh); *Breakfast Plays: The Girl in the Machine* (Traverse Theatre); *Flo, Thoughts Spoken Aloud From Above* and *Tristan Nightaway* (Òran Mór); *Uncanny Valley* (Ayr Gaiety/Edinburgh International Science Festival); *Molly Whuppie* and *Licketyleap* (Licketyspit); *The Silence of Bees* (The Arches); *The Hunted* (Visible Fictions); *Romeo and Juliet* (Open Book); *I Was a Beautiful Day* (Finborough Theatre/Tron Theatre); *Fast Labour* (West Yorkshire Playhouse/ Hampstead Theatre).

Television and film credits include: *Outlander* (Sony/Starz); *River City* (BBC Scotland); *Lip Service* (Kudos); *Closing the Ring* (Sir Richard Attenborough); *Doctors* and *Sea of Souls* (BBC).

About Traverse Theatre Company

Formed in 1963 by a group of passionate theatre enthusiasts, the Traverse Theatre was originally founded to extend the spirit of the Edinburgh festivals throughout the year. Today, under Artistic Director Orla O'Loughlin, the Traverse is proud to deliver its year-round mission of championing creative talent by placing powerful and contemporary theatre at the heart of cultural life – producing and programming urgent and diverse work spanning theatre, dance, performance, music and spoken word.

Through the work it presents, the Traverse aims to both entertain and stir conversation – reflecting the times and provoking crucial debate amongst audiences, inspiring them to ask questions, seek answers and challenge the status quo.

The Traverse has launched the careers of some of the UK's most celebrated writers – David Greig, David Harrower and Zinnie Harris – and continues to discover and support new voices, including Stef Smith, Morna Pearson, Gary McNair and Rob Drummond.

With two custom-built and versatile theatre spaces, the Traverse's home in Edinburgh's city centre holds an iconic status as the theatrical heart of the Edinburgh Festival Fringe every August.

Outside the theatre walls, the Traverse runs an extensive engagement programme, offering audiences of all ages and backgrounds the opportunity to explore, create and develop. Further afield, the Traverse frequently tours internationally and engages in exchanges and partnerships – most recently in India, New Zealand and Quebec.

'The Traverse remains the best new writing theatre in Britain.' *Guardian*

For more information about the Traverse please visit **traverse.co.uk**.

With thanks

The Traverse Theatre extends grateful thanks to all those who generously support our work, including those who prefer their support to remain anonymous.

Traverse Theatre Supporters
Diamond – Alan & Penny Barr, Katie Bradford
Platinum – Angus McLeod, Iain Millar, Nicholas & Lesley Pryor, David Rodgers
Gold – Carola Bronte-Stewart, Helen Pitkethly
Silver – Judy & Steve, Bridget M Stevens, Allan Wilson
Bronze – Barbara Cartwright, Alex Oliver & Duncan Stephen

Trusts, Foundations and Grants
Anderson Anderson & Brown Charitable Initiative
The Backstage Trust
Bòrd na Gàidhlig
British Council: UK/India 2017
The Cross Trust
The Dr David Summers Charitable Trust
Edinburgh Airport Community Board
The Educational Institute of Scotland
The Evelyn Drysdale Charitable Trust
The Foyle Foundation
The JMK Trust
Ponton House Trust
The RKT Harris Charitable Trust
The Robert Haldane Smith Charitable Foundation
The Russell Trust
The Santander Foundation
The Souter Charitable Trust
The Turtleton Charitable Trust
WCH Trust for Children

Traverse Theatre Production Supporters
Allander Print
Cotterell & Co
Paterson SA Hairdressing
Narcissus Flowers

Grant Funders

Traverse Theatre (Scotland) is a Limited Company (SC076037) and a Scottish Charity (SC002368) with its Registered Office at 10 Cambridge Street, Edinburgh, Scotland, EH1 2ED.

Traverse Theatre

The Company

Linda Crooks	Executive Producer & Joint Chief Executive
Stephen Dennehy	Box Office Supervisor
Isobel Dew	Administrator
Anna Docherty	Press & Media Officer
David Drummond	General Manager
Claire Elliot	Deputy Electrician
Sarah Farrell	Box Office Supervisor
Danielle Fentiman	Artistic Administrator
Ellen Gledhill	Development Manager
Tom Grayson	Box Office Manager
Rebecca Kirby	Deputy Box Office Manager
Rebecca Low	Project Development Assistant
Kath Lowe	Front of House Manager
Kevin McCallum	Head of Production
Ruth McEwan	Producer
Lauren McLay	Marketing & Communications Assistant
Suzanne Murray	Bar Café Manager
Victoria Murray	Head of Communications
Gareth Nicholls	Associate Director
Orla O'Loughlin	Artistic Director & Joint Chief Executive
Alice Pelan	Finance & Admin Apprentice
Julie Pigott	Head of Finance & Operations
Pauleen Rafferty	Payroll & HR Manager
Sunniva Ramsay	Creative Producer (Learning)
Renny Robertson	Chief Electrician
Tom Saunders	Lighting & Sound Technician
Dean Scott	Head Chef
Gary Staerck	Head of Stage
Kyriakos Vogiatzis	Marketing & Campaigns Officer
Miriam Wright	Box Office Supervisor

Also working for the Traverse

Grazyna Adrian, Eleanor Agnew, Charlotte Anderson, Lindsay Anderson, Shellie-Ann Barrowcliffe, Alannah Beaton, Emma Campbell, Hannah Cornish, Stephen Cox, Nicai Cruz, Rachel Cullen, Koralia Daskalaki, Amy Dawson, Rachel Duke, Andrew Findlater, Daniel Findlay Carroll, Sorcha Fitzgerald, Andrew Gannon, Laura Hawkins, Sunny Howie, Ian Jackson, Adam James, Nikki Kalkman, Neil Kean, Jonathan Kennedy, Sean Langtree, Fergus Lockie, Alan Massie, Kieran McCruden, Alison McFarlane, Kirsty McIntyre, Edwin Milne, Will Moore, Michael Murray, Carlos Navarro, Alex Palmer, Stephanie Ritchie, Lauren Roberts, Clare Ross, Jonathan Rowett, Theodora Sakellaridou, Kolbrun Sigfusdottir, Dylan Smith, Joanne Sykes, Linda Taylor, Elena Tirado, Rebecca Waites, Jessica Ward, Rosie Ward, Emma Whyte, Imogen Wilson, Sophie Wright.

GUT

Frances Poet

Acknowledgements

Thank you to Gary McNair for telling me to write the play and Zinnie Harris for championing it, shaping it and delivering it into the world.

For their support and input, Orla O'Loughlin, Kate Wasserberg, Vicky Featherstone, Caroline Newall, George Aza-Selinger, Rosie Kellagher, Davina Shah, Andrew Rosthorn, Viviene Cree, Kerry Dempsey, Lucianne McEvoy, Anita Vettesse, Lewis Howden, Anne Kidd, Irene MacDougall, John Kazak, Kirsty Stuart, George Anton, Lorraine McIntosh and Pete Collins.

Thanks to all the friends who have navigated the uncharted waters of parenthood alongside me, sharing their stories and fears, especially Hazel, Louise, Rachel, Tim and the NCTers, Heather and Jono, Andrew and Maggie, Beccy and Alex.

Ellie, who should always have a thank-you.

Peter and Elizabeth, who changed me by arriving into the world and let me run away to beautiful Cove Park to write the play even though they and Daddy were ill. And most of all to my live-in dramaturg (I know you hate the word) Richard, for his endless patience, support and love.

F.P.

For Janet and Roger,
who did it well and taught me how

Characters

MADDY, *thirties*
RORY, *thirties*
MORVEN, *sixties*
THE STRANGER…
   DAD
   CHARITY WORKER
   POLICE OFFICER
   COLLEAGUE
   GRIEVING STRANGER
   STONER
   NURSERY DAD
And JOSHUA

This text went to press before the end of rehearsals and so may differ slightly from the play as performed.

Maddy and Rory's Kitchen-Diner

MADDY *and* RORY, *just home from a romantic getaway* (*overnight bags by their feet*) *are telling* MORVEN *about their trip. They are like a double act, enjoying airing their good-humoured arguments for* RORY*'s mother.* MADDY *has the baby monitor in her hand and fiddles with it as they tell their story.*

MADDY. I'm telling you, it was like a maze.

RORY. A maze? It was a corridor with six doors off it.

MADDY. None of the doors had locks on them so –

RORY. They did have locks.

MADDY. Yes, old-fashioned turn-your-key-in-the-door-if-you're-going-out-for-the-day locks but not the usual self-locking mechanism that every other hotel in the world has –

RORY. I'd have booked us into a Premier Inn if I'd known the type of lock was the most important feature. You're the one who wanted a boutique hotel.

MADDY. And there was no en suite.

MORVEN. Oh that's a shame.

RORY. There were two bathrooms between four rooms. Big beautiful rooms with huge cast-iron baths and walk-in showers. Not some plastic cupboard with a toilet and leaky, push-button shower.

MADDY. And I drank too much wine with dinner.

RORY. We both did.

MADDY. So I wake up in the middle of the night bursting for a pee and I'm disorientated and I go out into this maze of doors.

RORY. Six. Six doors.

MADDY. Pat myself on the back for finding a bathroom. Empty my bladder and go back to the bedroom. And when I get into our room, I trip over what I think must be Rory's boots and Rory grunts something like 'What's happening?' and I say. Oh God, don't make me say it.

RORY. Maddy says, all sultry, 'It's the girl of your dreams.'

MADDY. And I go to get into the bed and Rory's on my side.

RORY. But I wasn't. I hadn't moved.

MADDY. And I say…

RORY. 'Hey baby, if you want me in this bed, you'd better budge over.'

MADDY. I should have just said, 'Move Rory' like I normally do but I was trying to be… Anyway Rory budges up so I slide into bed beside him and he says in this quite low growly voice.

RORY. 'You smell good.'

MADDY. Something like that. And it doesn't sound like him but I'm thinking he's putting on a silly sexy voice and so I say something like. Do we have to tell your mum this?

MORVEN. You've started now!

MADDY. So I said, 'Come on then if we're doing this.'

RORY. And she rolls in and caresses my head.

MADDY. Except it's not Rory's head. It's totally bald. And I yelp out, 'You're bald!'and reach for the light and –

RORY. She's gone into the wrong room. She's only got into bed with a total stranger.

MORVEN. Oh my word!

MADDY. And the worst thing is he thinks I came into his room deliberately.

RORY. 'It's the girl of your dreams.'

MADDY. Because I'm so shocked when I realise that I just jump up and run away without saying anything. No explanation.

So as far as he's concerned, it was all on until I discovered his bald head.

RORY. And then the next morning.

MADDY. At breakfast.

RORY. He's sitting opposite us, staring at Maddy.

MADDY. I'm trying not to make eye contact but he keeps looking at me. And then Rory abandons me.

RORY. I wanted more orange juice!

MADDY. And he comes up to me and in this low quiet voice he says. Oh God, you say it.

RORY. No, you. It's hilarious when you say it.

MADDY. He says... he says...

RORY. 'I can get a toupee if it's the hair that's the problem.'

MORVEN. No!

MADDY. He might have been joking. I'm not sure.

RORY. He wasn't joking. He passed her his number, scrawled on a napkin. 'I can get a toupee.'

MORVEN. Oh Maddy!

MADDY. I know! Trust me.

MORVEN. He must have thought Christmas had come early!

RORY. I'll bet!

MORVEN. You won't forget that trip in a hurry! Was it all excitement or did you manage to get a good rest too?

RORY. Well we spent a lot of time lying down...

MADDY *silences* RORY *with a look.*

MADDY. We had a lovely rest.

Thank you so much, Morven. It was the perfect way to spend our anniversary.

(*About the baby monitor.*) Is this working?

MADDY *passes the baby monitor to* RORY.

RORY. Yeah, thanks, Mum.

MORVEN. My pleasure. You should have stayed two nights.

RORY *passes back the baby monitor.*

RORY. Seems fine to me.

MORVEN. I told you we'd be fine. Though after what I've just heard, Rory would be wise to keep you at home from now on.

RORY. Too right. Anyway, careful what you offer. Now we know he'll settle for you, we'll have Granny sleepovers every Saturday night.

MADDY *is fiddling with the volume button on the monitor.*

MADDY. I can't hear anything.

RORY. He's sleeping. What's there to hear?

MADDY. How was he?

MORVEN. He's an angel.

RORY. Really?

MORVEN. Well, not so much at bedtime.

MADDY. Oh dear.

How many stories did he make you read?

MORVEN. I'm not saying.

RORY. I knew he'd have you wrapped round his little finger.

MORVEN. Tonight's bedtime did last quite a while.

MADDY. You are a saint.

MORVEN. Nonsense. It was good practice for when you're at the wedding on the 18th.

Right, well I'll get a move on. I've gone cold sitting here. Where's my big boy?

RORY. Night, Mum, thanks.

MORVEN. Night, Maddy. You look radiant.

MADDY. Thank you, Morven. It's done me a lot of good to get away – I really appreciate it.

MORVEN *gathers her belongings*.

Did he eat all his fish pie?

MORVEN. I decided to take him out for a treat tonight instead. Took him to our café.

MADDY. The one in the supermarket? What did he have?

MORVEN. You'll be cross with me.

MADDY. Of course I won't.

RORY. She will.

MADDY. Rory! What did he have?

MORVEN. Pizza with a side order of mixed vegetables.

MADDY. Mixed vegetables is good.

MORVEN. But he only ate the pizza.

In fact, he picked the cheese off the pizza and left the rest. And then he had jelly and ice cream but then as we were leaving, he spotted a chocolate rabbit so he had that as well.

RORY. At teatime? No wonder he was high as a kite when you were putting him to bed.

MORVEN. I tried to persuade him to go for the fish fingers but it all got bit panicked in the queue.

RORY. How come?

MORVEN. He needed a wee just as I was about to pay and I was carrying the trays with our meals and drinks. He was really desperate all of a sudden and I thought 'Oh God, how do I get out of this muddle?' But fortunately a nice man in the queue behind us offered to take him. He hadn't chosen his dinner yet so I took his empty tray and he took Joshua for a wee.

RORY. What?

MORVEN. Joshua was excited that he'd get to go into the boys' toilet instead of the ladies' with me.

MADDY. Which man?

MORVEN. Just a man.

RORY. Fuck's sake, Mum.

MADDY. Alright, calm down.

MORVEN. What have I said?

MADDY. I think Rory's just worried that you let a man we don't know –

RORY. A stranger.

MADDY. A stranger. Take Joshua.

RORY. A newly potty-trained three-year-old.

MADDY. Yes, thank you, Rory.

MORVEN. He was fine. He didn't have an accident or anything. His pants and trousers were dry so the man must have helped him.

RORY. Oh God.

MORVEN. And he'd definitely washed his hands because I checked when they got back.

RORY. Mum!

MADDY. Yeah, Morven, we don't care about whether Joshua washed his hands. I mean we do but. Who was the man?

MORVEN. Just a man. A nice kind man.

RORY. A total stranger.

MORVEN. Joshua was fine. He gobbled up his dinner, giggling and –

RORY. I'm going to wake him.

MADDY. Don't wake him.

MORVEN. I'm sorry if I've done it wrong. It was all a bit of a panic. I was holding two trays with his meal and my meal and drinks. I'd got my wallet out ready to pay. And when he needs to go, as you well know, you can't wait around.

MADDY. I know, Morven, but –

RORY. I'm going to wake him.

MADDY. Please don't.

RORY. Why's this guy offering to take a three-year-old to the toilet?

MADDY. I don't know.

MORVEN. I think he was a dad. Used to it.

MADDY. Did he have kids with him?

MORVEN. No, but. Maybe he was working away from home or... divorced, I don't know.

MADDY. Did he say that?

MORVEN. He didn't say anything really. Offered to help. Helped. Said goodbye. That was all it was. Totally innocent.

RORY. Lurking with no food on his tray at kids' teatime, just ready to leap into action. Anything could have happened. He could have taken Joshua. He could have stolen our son.

MORVEN. I'm sorry. I didn't think –

RORY. Clearly.

MADDY. Morven, it's fine. Joshua seemed fine?

MORVEN. Of course he did. He was his usual happy little self.

MADDY. Okay. That's fine then. Rory?

RORY. Yeah. Next time, it'd be better if you just took him yourself. He's still little and you think the world is full of helpful people but believe me, Mum, there's some evil shits out there.

MADDY. Look, Morven, why don't you get off. Thank you for everything. I'll call you, okay.

MORVEN. About the 18th?

MADDY. We'll see.

MORVEN. Okay. Night, Maddy. Night, love.

RORY doesn't answer. MORVEN *leaves. A moment between* RORY *and* MADDY.

RORY. Fucking hell.

MADDY. Why didn't she just put the tray down?

RORY. I'm going to wake him. I just want to hold him.

MADDY. Let him sleep.

RORY. What if something happened?

MADDY. It didn't. He brought him back. She said he seemed fine.

RORY. Okay.

A moment.

MADDY. Fuck it, you're right. Let's wake him.

A Soft-Play Centre

MADDY *sits at a café table facing out to the audience, watching Joshua playing on the soft-play equipment. At an adjoining table sits* THE STRANGER DAD, *also looking out towards the imagined play area.*

MADDY (*to offstage Joshua*). Go under it. Joshua, go under it. It's too big. That's right. Under it. Quickly, the little boy is trying to get past.

THE STRANGER DAD (*to his offstage son*). Wait a minute, Sam. Let the boy go first. Sam!

MADDY. Let the boy past, Joshua, and then you can go through. Watch how he does it and then you'll know how to. There. You go now. That's it. Well done.

THE STRANGER DAD (*to* MADDY). Sorry. My lad pushing past.

MADDY. Joshua was taking too long.

THE STRANGER DAD. He's the youngest of our brood so he's learnt muscling in is the only way you get a turn. Has your boy got brothers or sisters?

MADDY. No.

THE STRANGER DAD. No, 'not yet' or no, 'not ever'?

MADDY. Oh, um, 'not yet' probably. I'd like Joshua to have a brother or sister. My husband and I are both only children so no cousins or... which is a shame.

THE STRANGER DAD. We've got four.

MADDY. Wow.

THE STRANGER DAD. Our eldest is twelve. The first three came quickly then we had a little pause before we had Sam.

MADDY (*to offstage Joshua*). Joshua, stop licking it.

THE STRANGER DAD (*to offstage Sam*). No Sam, it's not a game. You can stop licking it too.

MADDY. It's covered in germs. Stop it, Joshua.

THE STRANGER DAD. Best buds now – in league against us.

MADDY. Joshua, no. Go and play in the balls. But don't lick them. Good boy.

THE STRANGER DAD. It's easier now three of them are at school.

MADDY. Is it?

THE STRANGER DAD. No, not really. Ferrying them about, nagging them to do their homework then worrying what they're looking at on their computer – not sure it ever does get easier.

MADDY. Oh dear.

THE STRANGER DAD. I'm Tony, by the way.

MADDY. Maddy.

THE STRANGER DAD. Maddy. Like in Maggie and Maddy – you read those? My eldest's favourite.

Or Maddy McCann. Sorry, don't know why I said that. Short for Madeleine?

MADDY. No. Madra. I hate it. My parents were in Spain when they were choosing names.

THE STRANGER DAD. Ah, Español! Yo vivía en España por un tiempo.

It means… 'mother', right?

MADDY (*to offstage Joshua*). Do you need a weewee, Joshua? Joshua? Are you sure? Stop holding yourself then, please.

THE STRANGER DAD. Don't let me put you off. Having more. I love having a whole brood.

MADDY. I read an article that said the worst amount of children to have in terms of parental happiness is three because you still try to have the same exacting standards you had with two, but it's just not possible. Whereas with four, you just cross your fingers and hope they all survive.

THE STRANGER DAD. That sounds pretty accurate.

MADDY. You must worry less, when there's four. It can't be the same amount of anxiety four times over? It would crush you, wouldn't it?

THE STRANGER DAD. You do relax a bit. You realise how robust the little blighters are.

MADDY. Are they though? Are they robust?

THE STRANGER DAD. I think so. They're going to get bumped and bruised. That's how they learn.

MADDY. Ahhhh look, our boys are cuddling.

THE STRANGER DAD. Firm friends.

MADDY. I think it's cuddling.

THE STRANGER DAD. You never can tell with boys.

MADDY (*to offstage Joshua*). That's right, gentle, boys. Ahh, nice cuddle.

THE STRANGER DAD (*to offstage Sam*). Are you alright, Sam? Um, I think –

MADDY (*to offstage Joshua*). Gentle, Joshua.

THE STRANGER DAD. I think he may actually be hurting Sam. Is he biting him?

MADDY. Joshua!

THE STRANGER DAD. He is. He's biting him.

MADDY (*to offstage Joshua*). Joshua, you stop biting that boy this minute.

THE STRANGER DAD. He's not letting go.

(*To offstage Joshua.*) Stop that. Oy, stop that.

MADDY (*to offstage Joshua*). Joshua!

THE STRANGER DAD (*to* MADDY). What's wrong with him?

MADDY *has no answer.*

(*To offstage Sam.*) It's all right, Sam. Come here and let me love it better.

MADDY (*to offstage Joshua*). You do not bite. Ever. Say sorry. Say sorry now. Don't walk away from me. Come here, Joshua, come back here.

THE STRANGER DAD. I know, love. That boy wasn't nice. Just come back out through that tunnel and I'll give you a cuddle.

MADDY (*to offstage Joshua*). If you don't come back here and say sorry, we are leaving straight away. Joshua. Joshua.

MADDY *frantically collects up her things to go.*

(*To* STRANGER DAD.) He's just really tired I think. He had a disturbed night. We woke him and brought him into bed with us so. It's our fault really. I'm so sorry.

Maddy and Rory's Kitchen-Diner

It's evening and RORY *is putting away toys, painstakingly.*
MADDY *is fiddling with the baby monitor.*

RORY. Do it again.

MADDY. Wah, wah, wah, wah, wah. Do you know what it is?

RORY. No.

MADDY. Is it from a song?

RORY. I doubt it.

MADDY (*about the baby monitor*). This is still playing up.
We're going to have to get a new one. Remember when I had
that 'Solar System' song from Joshua's KidsTV123 stuck in
my head. 'I am the sun, bah bah bah.' Stuck for days. Well
that was better than this. I think it might be a cat talking. I'm
not sure why. It must be from a cartoon or something.

RORY (*as if he might have an idea what it is*). Do it again.

MADDY. Wahwahwahwahwah.

RORY (*he's so close to knowing what it is*). Again.

MADDY. Wahwahwahwahwah. Do you recognise it?

RORY. One more time.

MADDY. Wahwahwahwahwah. Well?

RORY. Haven't a clue, you just look hilarious when you do it.

MADDY. Rory!

RORY. So how was Joshy today?

Monitor still in hand, MADDY *starts to tidy up.*

MADDY (*a bit cagey*). Fine. A bit tired maybe.

RORY. I spoke to Mum earlier.

MADDY. Oh yeah? Me too actually.

RORY. I know.

MADDY (*reading* RORY*'s expression*). I didn't want to worry you. I asked her not to mention it.

RORY. Joshua bit a kid?

MADDY. It's nothing to do with yesterday.

She chucks some bricks in a box.

RORY. I didn't say it was. (*About the bricks.*) Those don't go in there.

RORY *retrieves the bricks* MADDY *put in the wrong box.*

MADDY. It's just you got quite worked up and I didn't want to tell you anything that –

RORY. I got 'quite worked up' because my own mother made a spectacularly bad judgement call and put my kid in danger.

MADDY. But he's okay. He's absolutely fine. Kids bite each other. It's what they do. It was inevitable Joshua was going to do it at some point. He just chose today.

RORY. So why did you phone Mum about it?

MADDY. She's done it all before. She's gone through every stage with you.

RORY. What did she say? Was I a biter?

MADDY. You still are. On occasion.

A shared raised eyebrow.

She reassured me that all kids go through a biting phase and it wasn't anything to worry about. I asked her not to mention it to you. She said she wouldn't.

RORY. I am her son.

MADDY. And I'm her daughter.

RORY. In-law. Otherwise you and me've got a problem, kiddo.

MADDY. It was for her benefit. You were angry enough. I didn't want to add any fuel to –

RORY. I'm still angry, Maddy. If she hadn't done what she did, you wouldn't be worrying that our son biting is some sort of... cry for help.

MADDY. I'm not worrying. Kids bite.

RORY. I know that. Sarah at work says her daughter's nursery's like the fucking Hunger Games.

MADDY. Brutal.

They share a laugh. MADDY *puts down the monitor.*

I should have phoned you. You seem calmer than you were last night.

RORY. I checked Joshy this morning.

MADDY. What?

RORY. After he went to the loo. I got him to bend over and had a good look. There was no bruising or. Nothing to suggest he'd been, you know.

MADDY. What?

RORY. Penetrated or...

MADDY. Fuck. Rory! Fuck.

RORY. He was fine. I just needed to be sure.

MADDY. You actually thought...? I mean not just some weirdo who got a thrill from taking him. You actually thought Joshy might have been...? Physically...?

RORY. Yeah. Didn't you?

Something has broken for MADDY. *The world is a different place.*

Out of Space and Time

MADDY *is holding a canteen tray with tea on it*. THE
STRANGER *looms towards her.*

MADDY *feels threatened. She drops her tray. She bends down
to clear up the mess. When she looks up again* THE
STRANGER *has gone.*

The Supermarket Café

MORVEN, *just arrived, joins* MADDY *at a table. She arrives
in a flurry and kisses her.*

MORVEN. I've had such a to-do getting here. Traffic's terrible
at this time. It was so slow I got off the bus a stop early.
Suffice to say it sailed past me before I'd huffed and puffed
my way to my usual stop. Let's make it our usual time next
week, shall we? Where is that grandson of mine?

MADDY. I got us tea.

MORVEN. You're a treasure – thank you. Shall I be mother?

MORVEN *pours the teas.*

Where is Joshy? Are you hiding under the table, young man?

MADDY. He's at nursery.

MORVEN. Aren't you going shopping then?

MADDY. Not today.

MORVEN. There are much nicer cafés. This is perfectly good for
me and Joshy while you shop but if it's just the two of us…

MADDY. It's not.

MORVEN. Is everything alright?

RORY *enters.*

RORY. Sorry I'm late. Traffic was…

(*To* MADDY.) Hello, gorgeous.

Hi, Mum.

MORVEN. Hello, love. You're not in work today?

RORY. Yes and no. Don't look so worried. We just wanted to. Clear the air.

MORVEN. Oh. I didn't realise it was… unclear.

RORY. I'd like you to talk us through it. What happened when you brought Joshua here. Just so we understand exactly what happened.

MORVEN. Is Joshua okay? Has he said something? This isn't about that business with the biting –

RORY. It would just be helpful, Mum. Do you mind?

Does she have a choice?

MORVEN. Alright.

Well, I was standing over there. I was pushing two trays, one with my meal on it and one with Joshua's. I had my wallet in my hand. The woman in front was just finishing paying so it was my turn next.

RORY. Who was at the till? Was it that man there?

MORVEN. I don't know. Maybe. No, I think it was a woman.

RORY. And?

MORVEN. And then Joshua starts hopping about, holding himself. 'Granny Granny, I need to weewee.' And I said, 'I can't take you right now, Joshua, can you hold on just two minutes and then I'll take you.' And Joshua says, 'I'll try, Granny.' But he's hopping about, clutching at himself. 'Do you think you can hold on, Joshua, or is it about to come?' And then this man next to us says, 'Do you want me to take him? I haven't chosen my meal yet.'

RORY. What was the man doing before he said that? Was he in the queue or did he come over when he saw Joshua?

MORVEN. He was in the queue, I think. I hadn't noticed him until then but when I asked him if he was sure, I took his empty tray so he must have been in the queue.

MADDY. What did he look like?

MORVEN. He was just a normal-seeming man.

MADDY. How old?

MORVEN. I don't know. Not as old as me. Older than Rory. Smart, not wearing a suit but well presented. Jeans, a nice jumper maybe. Slim. Clean-looking. Polite.

MADDY. Can you see him here now?

MORVEN. No.

MADDY. You haven't looked.

MORVEN *looks around the room*.

MORVEN. No.

RORY. So you're in the queue and the man takes Joshua away. How long for?

MORVEN. Not long.

RORY. How long?

MORVEN. I don't know. I paid for the food and chose a table. I was just taking the food off the trays when they came back. It didn't feel long at all.

RORY. And then what?

MORVEN. I thanked him. Asked if Joshua had washed his hands. The man said he had and he hadn't even needed to remind him. But had helped him reach the soap. He said he was a very good boy. I told Joshua to say thank you and we said goodbye and ate our dinner.

RORY. Did the man get his meal then?

MORVEN. I don't know. Probably. Yes, I waved goodbye to him when we had finished ours.

RORY. Was he with anybody when he was eating his dinner?

MORVEN. Um, no. He was reading a book, I think.

MADDY. What book?

MORVEN. I've no idea. I stacked up our trays and we went home. That was it. That's everything.

RORY. Okay, thank you.

MORVEN. Is Joshua alright?

RORY. We think so. I mean physically he's not damaged but as Maddy pointed out that doesn't mean something didn't happen. We both feel a bit shell-shocked to be honest, Mum. Do you think that man could have done something to our boy?

MORVEN. No. No, I don't. Nothing about him seemed dangerous. I didn't get any bad vibes off him, no goosebumps or. I'm a good judge of character, Rory. You know I am. Always been able to trust my gut.

RORY *nods*.

RORY. Okay.

MADDY *studies* RORY.

It sounds like – it was a silly thing to do – but it sounds like it was innocent enough. I think we had a really lucky escape. I'm not trying to tell you off or...

Look, let's not talk about it again. It's water under the bridge. We love you and we are grateful for all you do for us and Joshua. Okay?

MORVEN *nods, chastened*. RORY *puts his coat back on*.

MADDY. You're not going?

RORY. I have to get to my meeting.

MADDY. That's it?

RORY. I'd much rather stay and drink tea with my two favourite ladies but I've got to get back.

Love you, Mum.

(*To* MADDY.) See you later.

RORY *exits. A moment.*

MORVEN. Goodness me. I feel a little shell-shocked myself after that. You could have warned me.

MADDY. Sorry.

MORVEN. I don't see how going over it like that helps. 'All the details.' I mean, what does he expect me to tell you? Can I 'see him here now?' What is this, some sort of Crimestoppers reenactment? He was a nice man, a friendly man trying to help. And if I'm wrong. If you really think something happened – ask Joshua. He's the only one who can tell you.

MADDY. I don't. We don't. Everything's fine.

A Public Toilet

MADDY *stands outside a toilet cubicle. The door is slightly ajar. She talks to Joshua who is the other side. While we may hear some audio of Joshua on the toilet, sing-songing, etc. Joshua does not respond to* MADDY's *questions. Any pauses come from* MADDY's *own thought process rather than a sense that she is hearing a response.*

MADDY. Try not to touch under the toilet seat, Joshua. No, no, you'll need to touch the seat to hold yourself up but try not to touch underneath the seat. It's just dirtiest under there, my darling. Are you done? Is it a poo? Okay, sweetheart. You take your time.

Joshua, when Granny took you out for your tea. And you had pizza and a chocolate rabbit. You went to a loo like this didn't you. While Granny was paying for the meal. A man brought you to the toilet. Was that... Was he a nice man? No, don't touch that please. It's dirty. It's for dirty things a bit like nappies but for mummies not babies. You went into the boy's toilet didn't you, with the man? Like you do with

Daddy. How much did the man help you? Or did he stand all the way out here like I'm doing so you can be a big boy and do it all by yourself? Have you finished your poo? Do you want me to come and wipe you? You're doing it yourself. Okay. That's right, pull that. You might need more than that little piece. Was there anybody else in the toilets when the man brought you? You don't need that much toilet paper, do you? Stop now, Joshua. That's too much. Stop. Okay, good. Just tear a smaller bit off that. It's trailing all over the floor. Get a smaller bit. Okay. Good boy. Did the man go to the toilet too when you did? Did you see his peepee? Did you touch it? Did you? Joshy, answer Mummy, please. Did you touch each other's peepees? Why are you covering your ears, sweetie? Is there something you want to tell Mummy? (*Desperate now…*) Joshy, why are you covering your ears?!

A breath. She composes herself.

Is Mummy being annoying? Yeah? You're sick of Mummy asking questions, is that it?

Okay, my love. Okay. Let's get your hands washed and get out of here.

Maddy and Rory's Garden

MADDY *is hanging out the washing.*

MADDY. Joshua, you're very quiet. What are you up to, mister? Come over here and help Mummy hang out the washing – you can play with the pegs.

Joshua doesn't come. Time passes. THE STRANGER CHARITY WORKER *enters.*

THE STRANGER CHARITY WORKER. Hello! Making the most of the good drying weather are you?

MADDY. Can I help you?

THE STRANGER CHARITY WORKER. Oooh, very businesslike. I need to take a leaf out of your book. I'm actually here on behalf of an animal-protection charity.

MADDY. How did you get in?

THE STRANGER CHARITY WORKER. Your little fella let me in.

MADDY. He's too small to reach the latch.

THE STRANGER CHARITY WORKER. Only a few millimetres off though, I'd say. He told me to come through.

MADDY. So you let yourself in?

THE STRANGER CHARITY WORKER. He was showing me his cars. He thinks the blue one is fastest but I'm sure it's the red.

MADDY. You've been playing cars with my son in our private garden?

THE STRANGER CHARITY WORKER. Well, yes.

MADDY. You think that's okay, do you? You think that's appropriate?

THE STRANGER CHARITY WORKER. I just had a wee chat with the lad.

MADDY. I could phone the police.

THE STRANGER CHARITY WORKER. Whoa. Can we just...? I have a badge.

MADDY. A total stranger talking to my child without making me aware of his presence.

THE STRANGER CHARITY WORKER. I'm not a stranger. I know the boy. Joe, is it? Johnny? I'm terrible with names. My niece goes to his nursery. Little Chloe. I pick her up on Thursdays – always have a laugh with the lad. He's a gutsy little fella, gives me high-fives that nearly knock my arm off.

MADDY. Chloe's uncle?

THE STRANGER CHARITY WORKER. We were introduced
in my sister's kitchen – Chloe's party...

MADDY. Oh God, I'm sorry. I didn't –

THE STRANGER CHARITY WORKER. You always give me
a big smile at drop-off.

MADDY. I didn't realise –

THE STRANGER CHARITY WORKER. Sorry to have
intruded.

MADDY. Give me a leaflet. I'll check it out. I'll make
a donation. A big donation. I'll do it straight away.

THE STRANGER CHARITY WORKER. Alright, love. Thanks
for your time.

Spirit broken, THE STRANGER CHARITY WORKER
leaves.

MADDY. Send our love to Chloe!

She's mortified.

Joshua, get over here now.

Maddy and Rory's Kitchen-Diner

RORY *is methodically organising toys.* MADDY *is in her
dressing gown, applying a cream to her upper chest and
underarm area.*

MADDY. Thanks a lot! I'm not a leper.

RORY. I just said I was happy over here. Tidying.

MADDY. I've tidied all of that.

RORY. You've picked them up off the floor. And dumped them
all in the red box.

MADDY. Yes. So it's tidy.

RORY. There's a system. Vehicles in the white box, construction toys in the red and any other plastic tat in the basket. He won't learn anything if everything's mixed up.

MADDY. If you're looking for a job, you can get that lock on the gate.

RORY. It's dark!

MADDY. You promised.

RORY. I'll do it at the weekend.

MADDY. You said that last weekend.

RORY. Alright. Bloody hell.

    RORY *continues tidying*.

MADDY. The first thing Joshy will do when he wakes up tomorrow is to empty everything out of the boxes again.

RORY. And I'll tidy it all up again tomorrow night. Doesn't bother me.

MADDY. So long as you don't have to sit next to your blotchy wife.

RORY. I didn't say that.

MADDY. Anyway, we all have yeast and stuff living on us. Even you.

RORY. Whatever you say.

MADDY. The doctor said. Yeast on the skin, microscopic spiders on our faces, microbes in our gut. All these strange things living in and on us and some are bad for you but some are actually good – that's why people drink those disgusting probiotic drinks to get good bacteria into their guts.

RORY. You're saying I should rub up against you to share your yeasty rash?

MADDY. Only if you want to…

    RORY *is not forthcoming*.

You have the same yeasts living on you – mine have just found a crack in my skin and it's caused an infection. A little sympathy rather than revulsion would be nice.

She has finished with the cream and replaced its lid.

Pass me the monitor will you.

RORY. I'm sympathetic.

He chucks her the monitor.

Just at a distance.

MADDY *listens for a moment to hear her son's breathing.*

MADDY. The doctor thinks we should contact the police about Joshua.

RORY. What?

MADDY. She said if we had any doubts –

RORY. You spoke to our doctor about it?

MADDY. I thought the rash might be stress-related. She asked.

RORY. You're not stressed. Thought your work was deadly quiet at the moment.

MADDY. That's why she asked about things at home.

RORY *processes this.*

RORY. He's fine. Joshua's fine.

MADDY. Is he?

RORY *has picked up a Fisher-Price Play and Learn Puppy and accidentally sets off the tune: 'It's a great big colourful world out there…'*

RORY. How do you stop this thing?

MADDY. You don't – you have to wait until it's finished.

RORY. God, this is the most annoying tune I've ever heard. No off switch at all? I'm going to have to take the batteries out.

MADDY. They're screwed in.

RORY. Who bought this evil thing?

MADDY. Your mum.

The tune finally finishes.

I took Joshua swimming today and the lifeguard was being cheeky with him. Normally Joshua can't get enough of it, giggling away, but today he wasn't having any of it.

RORY. He's allowed to have an off-day. He's allowed to find that cheesy lifeguard annoying.

MADDY. He keeps talking about his willy. 'Knock, knock. Who's there? Willy.'

He's touching it all the time, pulling at it, stretching it.

RORY. He's a little boy. Boys play with their –

MADDY. Do you know what he said in the changing rooms? 'Willy wank.' He said it over and over. 'Willy wank, willy wank, willy wank.' He was giggling like crazy and all I'm thinking is where did he hear the word 'wank'?

This is harder for RORY *to explain away...*

RORY. It's just a sound, isn't it? It sounds funny. He doesn't know what it means.

MADDY. How can you be so sure?

RORY *accidentally presses the tune button on the Fisher-Price Puppy again.*

RORY. Oh my God, this this is. Ahhhh.

The tune finally finishes.

Look I just know. Here in my gut.

MADDY. Did you 'just know' when you bent him over to check his bum wasn't...?

RORY. I was panicking.

MADDY. What's changed? We speak to your mum at the café and then it's like you've pressed an off switch in your brain. Facts gathered, Mother given a stern rebuke, worry-mode turned off. Everything back in its rightful place. Neat and tidy.

RORY. I overreacted. You said that yourself. You told me to calm down about it and now I have.

MADDY. So now you're one-hundred-per-cent sure, are you?

RORY. I know my boy. I'd know if something had happened to him. Every parental instinct in me says he's fine.

MADDY. And you trust that? Your 'parental instinct'?

RORY. What about you? You spend the most time with him. What does your gut say?

MADDY. I don't know. He's probably fine.

But what if he's not? What if something happened to our boy and we've waited nearly a week to report it?

RORY *accidentally presses the tune again.*

RORY. Oh my God, I'm going to rip this thing in two.

Over the monitor, the sound of Joshua crying.

MADDY. Shit. We've woken him.

RORY. Give him a minute, he'll settle.

MADDY. He sounds upset.

RORY. Fine, I'll go. You've got that cream on your hands. This lot's all sorted. It just needs to go in the white box.

RORY *goes to leave, stops.*

The GP only said that about the police because she doesn't know all the facts and she could see you were worried. Don't listen to her. Joshy's fine.

He exits.

MADDY *collects up the pile* RORY *made. She goes to put it into the white box. She changes her mind last minute and drops it all into the red.*

A Police Station

MADDY *stands with* THE STRANGER POLICE OFFICER, *Joshua is playing just out of sight.*

MADDY. Because I was told half-past.

THE STRANGER POLICE OFFICER. I know. I'm sorry. Shelley got held up. She's on her way.

MADDY. Shelley?

THE STRANGER POLICE OFFICER. The social worker. She'll be conducting the interview today.

MADDY. And she knows the right way to ask him because I tried but it was… I mean, how do you ask without putting something horrible in their heads?

THE STRANGER POLICE OFFICER. We're trained in this.

MADDY *is reassured.*

MADDY. I hope you won't think I'm wasting your time.

THE STRANGER POLICE OFFICER. Of course not.

MADDY. Because he looks happy enough playing there but he's more withdrawn. Since. I'm sure he is. I think he is.

THE STRANGER POLICE OFFICER. You're doing the right thing. How can we catch the bad guys if people don't tell us when bad stuff might have happened? It's good that you're here.

MADDY. Good. Thank you.

What will you do? If he says something happened?

THE STRANGER POLICE OFFICER. We'll deal with that if and when.

MADDY. Will you do a medical examination?

THE STRANGER POLICE OFFICER. Possibly not.

MADDY. Because we've left it too late?

THE STRANGER POLICE OFFICER. Most important thing first of all is to establish if anything happened.

MADDY. So if he says the man touched him, you'll do one? But if he says no, then we'll just trust that. Because we've checked and we can't see anything physically wrong but maybe we don't know what to look for?

THE STRANGER POLICE OFFICER. A medical examination can be traumatic in its own right so we want to avoid that if we can. We don't want to cause any more harm than we need to.

MADDY. Will asking questions harm him? If questioning, probing him is going to cause harm, I don't want to do it. My husband doesn't... I mean what if nothing happened?

THE STRANGER POLICE OFFICER. Let's hope it didn't.

MADDY. Yes.

THE STRANGER POLICE OFFICER. Here she comes. I'll take Joshua through now.

MADDY. What?

THE STRANGER POLICE OFFICER. Shelley's here. I'll take Joshua through for the interview.

MADDY. Without me?

THE STRANGER POLICE OFFICER. Yes.

MADDY. No. I'm coming with him.

THE STRANGER POLICE OFFICER. I'm sorry if this hasn't been explained already...

MADDY. No. I'm not having him go through this alone.

THE STRANGER POLICE OFFICER. It's standard practice. Trust us. We know what we're doing.

MADDY. No. I either come in with him or we go home. I'm not letting a couple of strangers lead him off into a room without me.

THE STRANGER POLICE OFFICER. We don't need parental consent to interview your son.

MADDY. What?

But I'm his mother. He doesn't know you. I don't know you. You can't speak to him if I don't want you to.

THE STRANGER POLICE OFFICER. As soon as you involved us, it became our responsibility. We have to investigate it, with or without your consent.

MADDY. I've changed my mind. He's fine. I don't think anything happened. He's been a bit tired. Not withdrawn. A bit tired. I've been projecting my worries on him. I made a mistake. I want to withdraw what I said.

THE STRANGER POLICE OFFICER. Look, it's too late for that.

MADDY. He's fine. Nothing happened. You don't need to talk to him.

THE STRANGER POLICE OFFICER. I'm going to take Joshua now. It'll be much easier on the little fella if you don't get worked up. Show him it's going to be okay.

(*To offstage Joshua.*) Now then, young man, you come on over here with me and I'll introduce you to Shelley.

THE STRANGER POLICE OFFICER *exits towards Joshua.*

MADDY *pulls on a smile and gives the offstage Joshua a little thumbs-up. She holds the smile until they are out of sight. Anxiety rises.*

Maddy and Rory's Kitchen-Diner

MADDY *and* MORVEN *sit opposite each other, a pot of tea in front of them.* MORVEN, *just arrived, is talking to* MADDY, *who is still in her PJs and looks like she hasn't slept.*

MORVEN. So I was ready to give up really. You know me and technology. But I mentioned it to my new friend, Jeff, who I met at the library that time. I think I told you about him. He used to be a collector. His thing was antique jewellery but he said it's the same skillset and he'd see what he could find. Anyway, I explained what I was looking for and how it had to be the eight-inch model from 1978 and that you had Miss Piggy so we were looking for Fozzy or Gonzo. And he said, why not Kermit? And I said I understood that finding an original Kermit was nigh-on impossible. And he said, 'Let me see what I can do.' And once he had the bit between his teeth, I knew he'd find one. He phoned me, I mean really it must have been, three, four hours later. And he had it! An original Kermit.

MADDY. An original? No.

MORVEN. Well, you have a look and see.

MADDY. You've got it here?

MORVEN *carefully retrieves a package from her bag.* MADDY *opens it, excited. It is a eight-inch plastic model of Kermit the Frog from The Muppets.*

Oh my God. Morven, how did you...? This must have cost you a... Oh look at him. He's glorious. Oh my goodness. I love it. Thank you so much.

She embraces a delighted MORVEN.

MORVEN. Is it right? Did I get it right?

MADDY. It's perfect. It's not even my birthday for months.

MORVEN. Well... I just wanted to get you something. To cheer you up.

MADDY. Thank you.

MADDY *concentrates on parcelling up Kermit in his layers of protective wrapping once more.* MORVEN *picks up the teapot.*

MORVEN. Shall I be mother?

She pours a cup of tea.

Oh it's cold.

MADDY. I wasn't expecting you.

MORVEN. Shall I make us another?

MADDY. Not for me.

MORVEN. How are you feeling? Work must be missing you.

MADDY. They're fine. It's quiet at the moment.

MORVEN. Is it a virus do you think?

MADDY. I don't know. Might just be that I haven't been sleeping very well.

MORVEN (*gesturing to Kermit*). Aren't you going to put him out?

MADDY. God no, Joshua would get his hands on him and pull his little head off the moment I looked away. I'll put him with the others in my chest.

MORVEN. That seems a shame.

The annoying tune of the Fisher-Price Puppy blasts out from the playroom.

Is that Joshy? I thought he'd be at nursery this morning.

MADDY. I kept him out.

MORVEN. Is he poorly too?

MADDY. No. I just thought we'd take a few duvet days together. A rest. Do us good.

MORVEN. Well, I'll just pop my head in then and say hello. I want to tell him about this farm Jeff's told me about that I think we'll take him to when you're at Rory's friends' wedding.

MORVEN *goes towards the playroom*. MADDY *stands in front of her, blocking her way*.

MADDY. No.

MORVEN. Oh. Well, I suppose the farm can be a surprise.

MADDY. I don't want you taking him.

MORVEN. Are you going to take him with you to the wedding?

MADDY. I don't care about the wedding. Who is this Jeff? I don't know who he is. I don't want him near Joshua.

MORVEN. Jeff doesn't have to come if you –

MADDY. I don't want you near Joshua.

MORVEN. What?

MADDY. That sounds… I don't mean… I just don't think I'll be able to breathe if I let him go with you, Morven. You're too trusting. I don't think you see the world as it really is.

MORVEN. You're punishing me. For what happened at the café.

MADDY. Honestly I'm not.

MORVEN. Rory said Joshua was fine.

MADDY. I went to the police. They took Joshua into a room all rigged up with cameras and interviewed him without me.

MORVEN. Rory told me.

MADDY. Did he? I asked him not to.

MORVEN. He was upset about it.

MADDY. I know.

Do you also know what they said afterwards? That there wasn't enough evidence to take it further. I said, 'Okay, good. So you don't think anything happened?' They said they couldn't say that. That we'd never know. That sometimes we have to live, not knowing. That man might have touched Joshua sexually or he might have got Joshua to touch him or he might just have had a really good look at my boy and used it to fuel his fantasies when he got home.

MORVEN. Or he might just have helped him go to the toilet.

MADDY. But none of us will ever know, will we?

MORVEN. I'm sorry. I'm sorry I let Joshua go with a stranger.

MADDY. That is the first time you've said that.

MORVEN. In my day, we trusted people. We knew there were some bad apples but we thought most people were good.

MADDY. Maybe that's why so many children were abused, Morven. In the church, in schools, in children's clubs, in care, in hospitals.

MORVEN. I didn't have my mum either when I became a mum. I couldn't have raised Rory without the support of my neighbours, shopkeepers who would keep an eye out while I dashed out here or there, old folk who would give him 'what for' if he was up to something he shouldn't. I don't know how your lot get through it. How can you raise a child in a world where everybody you meet could be the sort of man you're talking about?

MADDY. We put our meal trays down when our young children need a wee, we don't dash here or there while a stranger keeps an eye out. We stay close to them, we watch them, we keep them safe.

MORVEN. I'll keep him safe. I'll never do anything like that again.

MADDY. I just don't trust you with him any more, Morven. I'm sorry.

MORVEN. This is madness.

MADDY. It's the way it is.

MORVEN. I'm his only grandparent.

MADDY. You think I don't know that?

MORVEN. I held you. On your wedding day, I held you and I said 'You're my daughter now.'

MADDY. I know.

MORVEN. I wasn't being sentimental. It wasn't the champagne. I meant that.

MADDY. I know.

MORVEN. Right. Well, I'll go then.

MADDY. Yes.

MORVEN. This is very hurtful.

MADDY. I'm sure.

MORVEN *starts to go. Then stops.*

MORVEN. I'll have that back, I think.

MADDY. What?

MORVEN. I bought it. I went to a lot of effort to get it. I'll take that back please.

MADDY. Kermit?

MORVEN. Yes.

MADDY. There's no need –

MORVEN. I think there is. Give me it, please. Give me Kermit.

MADDY. No. You're being spiteful.

MORVEN *reaches for it. A little tug of war.*

MORVEN. Give it to me.

MADDY. You gave it to me.

MORVEN. I want. It. Back.

MADDY. Let go, you'll break it.

MORVEN. I. Don't. Care.

MADDY. Fine.

MADDY *lets go of it,* MORVEN *stumbles backwards a little. The two women look at each other.*

Out of Space and Time

MADDY *is alone.* THE STRANGER *arrives, casting dark, distorted shadows. He takes a step towards* MADDY. *And another.* MADDY *backs away from him.*

Maddy and Rory's Kitchen-Diner

MADDY, RORY *and* RORY*'s colleague,* THE STRANGER COLLEAGUE, *sit round the table eating their meal. They are in the middle of a heated argument.*

MADDY. A witch-hunt? How can you possibly say that?

THE STRANGER COLLEAGUE. It's all predicated on the evidence of a group of women who attended Duncroft Approved School. But their stories don't hold up. This is delicious by the way.

MADDY. Thank you. But there have been hundreds of cases against him. Children, women…

RORY. Corpses.

THE STRANGER COLLEAGUE. Where's the hard evidence?

RORY. Well the corpses aren't saying much, it's true.

MADDY. But the women are!

THE STRANGER COLLEAGUE. And they all stand a chance to profit from it. How can you trust witness testimony when there's a financial incentive linked to it? And who's paying out the compensation?

MADDY. Savile's estate presumably.

THE STRANGER COLLEAGUE. I'll tell you who – the bloody NHS!

MADDY. But whoever's paying, that doesn't change the fact –

THE STRANGER COLLEAGUE. Your wife is a good cook –
he said you were.

RORY. Where are you getting all this? Steve is like a magnet
for conspiracy theories. It's a running joke in the office.

THE STRANGER COLLEAGUE. This academic I met at Alex
and Bec's wedding who specialises in moral panics. You'll
have seen him. The really tall bloke with the bow tie.

RORY. We didn't…

THE STRANGER COLLEAGUE. Cracked that joke partway
through the best man speech about –

RORY. We weren't there.

THE STRANGER COLLEAGUE. What? Oh yeah. I forgot you
didn't make it.

RORY *throws* MADDY *a quick look.*

RORY. Couldn't sort childcare.

THE STRANGER COLLEAGUE. Such a shame. It was a
cracking do.

Anyway this guy's building an archive of data from a lawyer,
who's dead now, but who blogged under the name Anna
Raccoon. And you can be as outraged as you like – but her
hard drive proves that the Duncroft girls cooked up their
stories about Savile on Facebook and Friends Reunited.

MADDY. I find the idea that women scheme and make up
stories about rape very offensive.

THE STRANGER COLLEAGUE. I tell you what's offensive.
Spending millions of pounds investigating decade-old
harassment claims when women's refuges are being closed
for lack of funds. Or pouring money into investigating the
activities of a creepy dead man while hundreds of thousands
of kids live in poverty.

Through the monitor we hear a crackle. MADDY *holds it to
her ear.*

RORY. Is he still not asleep?

MADDY. He had a late nap.

RORY. He's not sleeping as well since he's not been going to nursery.

MADDY. He had a late nap. It's nothing to do with nursery.

RORY *gives a dubious look.*

What? We spent three hours at the park. He is getting loads more exercise and fresh air than he ever used to at nursery.

Another crackle from the monitor. This time we hear Joshua's voice sing-songing:

JOSHUA (*on monitor*). 'Muuuuummeee, Muuuummmeee!'

RORY (*to the* COLLEAGUE). Maddy decided to take a sabbatical from work. To spend more time with Joshy. So his routine's changed a fair bit.

MADDY. He's loving it. And so am I. You only get them for such a short time. Children. Blink and you've suddenly missed their whole childhood.

Another crackle and Joshua's voice.

JOSHUA (*on monitor and perhaps from off too*). Daaaaaaaaaaaadeeeeeeeee, I'm thirsty.

RORY *gets up and fills a sippy cup of water.*

THE STRANGER COLLEAGUE. I think that's an amazing thing to do. All the adventures you can have together. He'll remember that forever.

RORY. I'll take this up.

THE STRANGER COLLEAGUE. Let me. Be great to meet the little chap. Say hello.

MADDY *gets up abruptly.*

RORY. That's okay isn't it, Maddy?

A change.

MADDY. If you go near my son. You paedophile-loving fuck. I will rip your heart out.

Back in the room. All as before.

RORY. Maddy?

MADDY. Of course. I'll come up with you.

She, all smiles, and THE STRANGER COLLEAGUE *go to leave for Joshua's room.*

Maddy and Rory's Kitchen-Diner

RORY *is washing up.* MADDY *is on the sofa fiddling with the baby monitor.*

MADDY. This thing still isn't working properly. Rory?

No answer.

You're cross with me.

RORY. I'm not cross with you.

MADDY. You've barely spoken to me since your colleague left.

RORY. Steve, his name is Steve. I'm clearing up.

MADDY. I've said I'll do it tomorrow.

RORY. I'm fine.

MADDY. What did you think of all that bollocks he was spouting about Savile?

RORY. I think he gets kicks from deliberately swimming upstream against public opinion.

MADDY. Totally.

RORY. But to be fair, that's just because he thinks the world should make decisions based on cold hard facts rather than hysteria and fear. If you get over the way he chooses to make his argument, he's actually got a point.

MADDY. I didn't like him.

RORY. I know.

MADDY. Sorry. But I didn't.

RORY. He's my friend, Maddy. And a colleague. I have to work with him every day.

MADDY. Doesn't mean I have to like him.

RORY. Of course not. I just won't make him part of our lives.

Pointing at some leftovers.

What should I do with this?

MADDY. Cling-film it and put it in the fridge. Joshy and I can eat it for our lunch.

RORY *goes to put away the leftovers but stops at* MADDY*'s question.*

Why did he want to see Joshua?

RORY. He wanted to meet him.

MADDY. It's a bit odd isn't it? Total stranger wanting to spend time with a three-year-old at bedtime.

RORY. He's not a stranger. He's my pal.

MADDY. He's a stranger to me.

RORY. But not to me.

MADDY. Well, most cases of child abuse and murder happen with people who are known to the parents.

RORY. Whoa, how did we get from here to there?

MADDY. This bloody monitor doesn't work.

RORY. Let me see.

RORY *walks over to* MADDY *and takes the monitor from her. He places it on the floor and stamps his foot on it.*

MADDY. Rory! What did you do that for?

RORY. He's three years old. He can call for us by name. He can get out of bed and come and see us. What the fuck do we need a baby monitor for?

MADDY. You could have just said that. You'll wake Joshua stomping on things like that.

RORY. What's going on, Maddy? First the police when I told you categorically we didn't need to involve them, then your sudden sabbatical and now this. What's going on with you? Where is this coming from?

MADDY. –

RORY. Talk to me. I can't bear it when you block me out.

MADDY. I'm not blocking you –

RORY. You are. Just like you did when we first met.

MADDY. When my mum had just died?!

RORY. You were so worried your grief would scare me away that you buried it. And it didn't lift until you started talking to me about her.

MADDY. 'It lifted' when I went to my group actually.

RORY. Alright. Fine. Either way, burying how you're feeling is not useful. Talk to me. Is it because of the fallout with my mum? Is that what's making you...

MADDY. Don't go over that again.

RORY. You miss her. I know you do.

MADDY. Of course I do.

RORY. Joshy does too.

MADDY. I know.

RORY. So sort it out. Make it up with her.

MADDY *doesn't respond. Points to the leftovers.*

MADDY. That needs covering now or it won't be fit for Joshy to eat.

Angry, RORY *storms away.* MADDY *puts her head in her hands and takes a deep breath.*

RORY *returns carrying cling film. Only it's not* RORY. *It's* THE STRANGER. *He tears off a bit of cling film and covers the leftovers.* MADDY, *sensing* RORY*'s presence but not looking, speaks to him.*

Don't be angry with me. I don't know why I'm… It's like I opened a door in my mind and now I can't shut it again.

THE STRANGER *takes the leftovers off. It's* RORY *who emerges.*

RORY. What did you say?

MADDY *looks at him.*

MADDY. I just said –

The broken monitor on the floor starts to crackle.

Bloody hell. It lives!

The broken monitor crackles again. MADDY *picks it up. An odd sound emerges from it – wahwahwahwahwahwah.*

That was the sound. Rory, did you hear it?

RORY. What sound?

MADDY. The 'wahwahwahwah' sound!

RORY. Not this again.

MORVEN *appears from the most unlikely of places.*

MORVEN. 'Charley and I were in the park.'

MADDY. Morven?!

MORVEN. You remember, Rory. 'Then this man came up and said would I like to see some puppies and – '

RORY*'s remembered it now.*

RORY (*in an uncanny impression of the 1973 Public Information Broadcast*). 'And I said "yes" and I was going to go but Charley stopped me.'

MORVEN. That's the one.

The baby monitor crackles again – wahwahwahwahwah. MADDY *drops it.*

RORY. 'Charley says never go anywhere with men or ladies you don't know.'

MADDY. I wasn't expecting you, Morven.

MORVEN. I wanted to introduce you to my new friend Jeff.

MADDY. It's very late –

The Fisher-Price Puppy, strewn on the floor, starts its tune though it hasn't been touched.

The happy song morphs into the voice of THE STRANGER *– 'I'm going to take Joshua now.'*

What the...?

And again – 'I'm going to take Joshua now.'

RORY. That bloody thing.

MADDY. Did you hear that?

RORY *and* MORVEN *act as though nothing out of the ordinary is happening.*

RORY. Mum, you do realise you gave us the world's most annoying toy.

MORVEN. Joshy loves it.

And again – 'I'm going to take Joshua now.'

MADDY. Are you hearing this?

RORY. Somebody needs to rip the batteries out.

THE STRANGER*'s voice can be heard again, this time from the other side of the room. 'He's a gutsy little fella. He's a gutsy little fella. He's a gutsy little fella.'*

MADDY. Can you hear his voice? Where's it coming from?

RORY. Whose voice? Maddy?

MADDY *searches for it, stopping at* MORVEN*'s handbag.*

MADDY. It's coming from your bag.

MORVEN. I very much doubt it.

MORVEN *starts to empty her bag, passing things to*
MADDY *including a chocolate rabbit and a* Jim'll Fix It
medal. Finally, she passes out the Kermit from earlier.
MADDY *holds it to her ear. Joshua can be heard crying.*

MADDY. It's Joshy, he's upset. I'll go to him.

RORY. He's fine.

MORVEN. His usual happy self.

MADDY *goes to check on Joshua.* THE STRANGER *is in
front of her, blocking her way. He hums the* Jim'll Fix It
theme tune.

THE STRANGER. Ba baaa bu bu bu, ba ba ba ba ba ba ba ba
bu bu.

MADDY *stops in her tracks. She stares at him and breathes.*

Now then.

MORVEN. Hello, Jeff.

RORY. Steve!

THE STRANGER. I'm Tony.

MORVEN. Just a man. A nice, kind man.

THE STRANGER. Chloe's uncle.

RORY. My pal. I work with him every day.

THE STRANGER *leans in close to* MADDY *and whispers…*

THE STRANGER. It'll be much easier on the little fella if you
don't get worked up.

MADDY. WHO ARE YOU?!

Maddy and Rory's Kitchen-Diner

It's the middle of the night. MADDY *has emptied a toolbox and is rifling through it.* RORY *enters and puts the light on.*

RORY. What on earth?

MADDY. Where are the screws?

RORY. What are you doing?

MADDY. Where are the fucking screws?

RORY. What's going on?

MADDY. I'm putting the lock on the gate.

RORY. It's 3 a.m.

MADDY. I can't sleep.

RORY. Maddy...

MADDY. I'm just doing the job you said you'd do. But there are no fucking screws.

RORY. It's the middle of the night. You're going to wake Joshua.

MADDY. It needs doing.

RORY. I'll do it. I've said I'll do it.

MADDY. Will you though?

RORY. I'll do it. I promise.

MADDY. We have to keep him safe.

RORY. You need to get on top of this, Maddy. Talk to some other mums, join a group or a class or. You need to... I want my Maddy back.

MADDY. I've not gone anywhere.

RORY. Come back to bed.

(*Soft now, playful.*) There's better things we can do if you can't sleep.

MADDY. I had this awful dream.

RORY. You should have woken me. It's okay. Everything's okay.

MADDY. Promise you'll do the lock.

RORY. First thing. I promise.

A Community Hall

THE GRIEVING STRANGER *takes us all in before addressing us*. MADDY *watches*.

THE GRIEVING STRANGER. She was a right potty-mouthed thing. Not just in her teens. Even as a little lass. We're walking along the canal this one time, pointing at every bicycle that whizzed passed us, stopping to pat every dog. Everybody else in a hurry but us. And she sees these wild poppies and she walks up to them and touches them, ever so gently. Looks up at me and smiles and says 'Come here, Daddy. Look at these pretty buggers.' Couldn't have been more than three or four. Pretty buggers. Makes me smile every time I think of that.

One more thing I want to tell you. Then I'll shut up. Thought of it the other day. We were on the floor, I think. Been wrestling or tickling or… Mucking about. She holds me tight and she says, 'If anybody ever hurts you, Daddy, I'll make them dead.' Don't know where she'd picked that up from. But she said it so serious like. Solemn. A promise. And I gave her some spiel about not a nice thing to say that and nobody would hurt me. But I remembered it the other day. Came to me like a punch in the gut and I thought. I wish you had, lassie. I wish you had made them dead. Because losing you. Losing you hurt me more than anything else ever could.

A Community Hall

After the meeting. MADDY *goes to leave.* THE GRIEVING STRANGER *catches up with her.*

THE GRIEVING STRANGER. How did you find it?

MADDY. Um, I…

THE GRIEVING STRANGER. First time's always difficult.

MADDY. It's not my first time.

THE GRIEVING STRANGER. Do you know, I thought your face was familiar. You used to come. A good few years ago now.

MADDY. Yeah.

THE GRIEVING STRANGER. Your mum, wasn't it? Cancer?

MADDY. Yeah. Eight years ago.

THE GRIEVING STRANGER. You're missing her? Or are you here for somebody else?

MADDY. –

THE GRIEVING STRANGER. Oh pet, I'm sorry.

Who?

MADDY *shakes her head.*

You know I really think it helps to say it. That's what this is for. I would make it a rule that newcomers have to say at least who they've come for. Because the relief when they do. Pain yes. But it's the beginning of starting to feel better. But they don't like rules here. Fair enough. You want to tell me?

Something builds. The world of the nightmare hasn't left MADDY.

MADDY. –

THE GRIEVING STRANGER. That's okay if you don't want to say… You take your time. Only you can –

MADDY. My son.

THE GRIEVING STRANGER. Oh hell.

MADDY. A stranger took him.

THE GRIEVING STRANGER. There are no words.

He holds her. She lets him. Gives in to it. This is the comfort she needed. The world of her nightmare has abated.

Tell me something about your son. A memory.

MADDY. I ought to go.

THE GRIEVING STRANGER. How about his first word? Please.

MADDY. Moon.

THE GRIEVING STRANGER. How lovely.

MADDY. He was only nine months. We'd been reading lots of stories with moons in them – *Goodnight Moon* and *Room on the Broom* and we were watching this cartoon together and there was a huge moon, filling the whole screen and he just, clear as anything, just said 'Moon.'

THE GRIEVING STRANGER. My daughter's first word was car. Didn't come out right. She said 'Gog'. Really insistent. 'Gog' and she'd point at whatever car was passing. 'Gog, gog!'

Did your mum get to meet him?

MADDY *shakes her head, upset.*

They're together now though. In heaven. Looking down at us and wondering what all the fuss is about.

MADDY. I can't do this.

She makes to leave.

THE GRIEVING STRANGER. I'll pray for your son.

MADDY *stops, turns back.*

MADDY. Please don't.

THE GRIEVING STRANGER. Sorry?

MADDY. No, I'm sorry. I'm so sorry.

THE GRIEVING STRANGER. I don't understand.

MADDY. Don't make me –

THE GRIEVING STRANGER. I've upset you. I didn't mean –

MADDY. My son's not dead!

THE GRIEVING STRANGER. What?

MADDY. I've been feeling this terrible sense of… I wanted to be around people who might understand. He's living and breathing and with his daddy at home but I am so terrified something bad is going to happen to him.

THE GRIEVING STRANGER. Why would you say he was dead?

MADDY. I didn't. Just that he's who I was here for. And he is.

THE GRIEVING STRANGER. This isn't a joke. Our grief isn't an entertainment.

MADDY. I know. I'm sorry.

THE GRIEVING STRANGER. So what? You came to make yourself feel better? You're feeling a little lost, a little neurotic and thought being with us would be the perfect medicine. Because while our hearts are breaking, your son is safe at home.

MADDY. I… I…

THE GRIEVING STRANGER. You shouldn't come here again.

MADDY *starts to leave. Stops.*

MADDY. It didn't make me feel better. How could it? Listening to Alice who'll never know what happened to her son the night he celebrated his A-level results and Sarah's sister who killed herself because some pervert fuck assaulted her at her ballet class when she was ten and you… You're stuck at exactly the same place you were eight years ago. Grieving for your daughter like you lost her yesterday. It DOESN'T help. It makes me even more terrified. How do I keep him safe? In a world where such horrible things can happen?

Everybody tells me to trust my gut but unless there's a probiotic that I can drink that will help my gut tell me what the fuck it's thinking, I don't know what to do. My gut and the world feel the same to me, unknowable and crammed full of strangers. And there's no way of knowing which ones will do me good and which ones will do me harm.

A silence.

I'm sorry. I'm going.

She starts to leave. THE GRIEVING STRANGER *catches her arm.*

THE GRIEVING STRANGER. You can keep him safe. Be vigilant. Keep your eyes wide open and most importantly... teach him. Your son. My daughter got in a car with a man she didn't know to save herself the twenty-pound taxi fare home. It was up to me to teach her not to do that. I failed her. Don't fail your son. Teach him.

Maddy and Rory's Kitchen-Diner

RORY *has just returned home from work and is standing with his bag still in his hand.* MADDY *is in the middle of telling him a story. She is elated.*

MADDY. See that's the thing with the climbing frame for the older children. None of the parents are watching. If they're even in the park. The big kids are left just to get on with it. But there's the occasional parent, like me, hovering with a little one who's too small for it really. I kept trying to persuade Joshy to stay in the little climbing area but of course he wants to be with the big boys. So I'm watching Joshua, helping him up this ladder, one rung at a time but I'm also watching this girl who's balancing on the monkey bars like she's on a trapeze. She's graceful, like a cat. And totally fearless. I'm looking round to see if anybody else is watching her. I half expect to see some father dressed like a ringmaster because surely this girl is from the circus. And I'm encouraging Joshua, lifting him down when he gets nervous. But all the time I'm watching this beautiful girl. And then she loses her footing and just drops through the bars. Still graceful. Anybody else would catch their arm on the way down but her arms are close to her body, rigid. And Joshua's down so I take a side-step right and. I catch her.

I caught her.

And she looks up at me – a total stranger – and smiles. And a couple of the parents gasp and then one of them shouts 'well done' and starts clapping. And two or three other parents join in and they are all clapping. Applauding me. And I set the girl down and she runs off, this lovely little thing, not a bump on her.

RORY. You caught her?

MADDY. She was light. A waif of a thing. And she landed so beautifully. It was almost like a dance. Like we'd practised it.

RORY. Well done.

MADDY. I had my eyes wide open and I caught her. I've been walking round with a smile on my face all day.

RORY. Where's Joshua?

MADDY. All bathed and in his PJs watching his fifth Fireman Sam.

RORY. I thought we were limiting it to one a day.

MADDY. We are but I wanted to be able to tell you my story. One night won't hurt.

RORY. Good.

MADDY. Dinner's ready – just need to cook the fillet steak.

RORY. Did you say fillet steak?

MADDY. I saw a pregnant lady today and I felt a teensy bit jealous. First time.

RORY. Really?

MADDY. Don't go getting any ideas. I'll put Joshua to bed quickly and we can enjoy our evening.

RORY. How quickly? Shall I start cooking the steaks?

MADDY. Go for it.

RORY. Shall we see Mum on Sunday? An olive branch.

Is the world of MADDY*'s nightmare going to come back?*

MADDY. Maybe. That could be nice.

Will you sort the lock? Before you start the steaks.

RORY. Of course. I'll do it now.

Any echo of the nightmare has gone.

MADDY. A kid pointed at me in the park after I caught the girl and called me 'hero lady'. Then Joshua and I played superheroes all afternoon. It was a perfect day.

RORY. SuperMum.

MADDY. That's me.

Maddy and Rory's Kitchen-Diner

*The outline of Joshua, snuggled in blankets, on the sofa. Kids'
TV plays quietly.* THE STRANGER *sits watching him, a beer in
his hand.*

MADDY *enters, arms full of various shopping bags. She goes
straight to the fridge and unpacks various bundles of food. She
still hasn't looked at* THE STRANGER.

MADDY. I'm back. There's this amazing new fishmonger's next to the art shop. I'm afraid I got a bit carried away. Then I've been worrying all the way home that it would spoil before I could get it in the fridge. It's baking out there. I also nipped into that beautiful kids' clothes shop. You know the boutiquey one that is crazy expensive. Anyway, they had a sale on and I got the most gorgeous yellow shorts for Joshua. And a lightweight coat that's the brightest orange you've ever seen.

She looks over at the TV.

You've not got the TV on? In this weather. Rory! You should be outside.

She finally looks up at THE STRANGER, *gets a real fright and positions herself between him and Joshua.*

Who are you?

THE STONER STRANGER. Sorry, I didn't know whether to interrupt or –

MADDY. Where's Rory?

THE STONER STRANGER. He went outside to turn off the hosepipe. He's been out there quite a while so I don't know if there's a problem or.

MADDY. Are you a friend of Rory's?

THE STONER STRANGER. No. I'm er. No.

MADDY. What are you doing in my house? Why are drinking beer in my house?

THE STONER STRANGER. There was a… I don't know whether you want your husband to tell you. There was a thing outside with the kid and a car.

MADDY. What? What do you mean?

THE STONER STRANGER. The kid got out of your back gate and took his bike down the road. I was standing outside my pal's house having a smoke and there was this old biddy pulling out of her drive and she didn't see him so.

MADDY. Did he get knocked down? Did she hit Joshua?

THE STONER STRANGER. Nah. I, um, I managed to get to him in time so. Your husband invited me in for a beer. As a thank-you or whatever. The little dude was a bit shaken up but the TV calmed him down so. He fell asleep on my knee actually so I lifted him onto to the sofa. Hope that was –

MADDY *goes to Joshua, inspects him then scoops him up into her arms, and exits carrying him bundled up in the blankets, all the time eying* THE STONER STRANGER *with suspicion and contempt.* THE STONER STRANGER *continues to swig his beer.*

RORY *enters from the garden, from the knees down he is wet and muddy.*

RORY. I'm sorry about that. It's bloody drenched out there. It was just cascading out of the paddling pool. Bloody thing. When I heard Joshy screaming I just dropped everything. I've been trying to ladle some of the water into the flower beds, stop it totally waterlogging the lawn. I still can't believe he managed to get through the gate. Anyway, I definitely need a swig of that beer now.

He picks up an open beer he left on the side. Raises it to THE STONER STRANGER.

Cheers man. You. You did a really good thing today. Thank you. Really.

Thank you.

THE STONER STRANGER. I was just in the right place at the right time, I guess. Your wife –

RORY. Oh God, Maddy. She's going to go / I mean, she will not react well to this. So what time are we now?

MADDY *re-enters. She hovers by the door where* RORY *cannot see her.*

If she gets back while we're still, can we maybe not mention it? She's been a bit overprotective with Joshy recently so… probably best not to feed her worries on that front. I'm going to put that fucking lock on the gate. That's the first thing. Anyway, look, sorry – I'm still feeling a bit shaken up. My thoughts are all over the place. You don't need to worry about any of that. Thank you… what's your name again? Sorry I…

THE STONER STRANGER *looks over at* MADDY. RORY *follows his gaze and sees* MADDY *for the first time.*

Maddy! You're back.

They lock eyes. THE STONER STRANGER *watches them.*

Out of Space and Time

MADDY*'s nightmare world is raging. Each and every one of Joshua's toys crackles with menace.* THE STRANGER *walks towards her.* MADDY *seems to flee but returns a moment later, full of purpose and carrying a car seat which she places firmly in the centre of the room between her and* THE STRANGER. *He backs away.*

Maddy and Rory's Kitchen-Diner

RORY *is just home from work, bag in hand.* MADDY *is full of nervous energy. Joshua's car seat sits prominently in the room. It shouldn't be there.*

RORY. What's wrong?

MADDY. Nothing's wrong. Come in. Sit down.

How was your day? I never remember to ask you about your day. Joshua's asleep. We can talk. I know it's early but he was… shattered.

How's what's-his-name? Still banging on about conspiracies?

RORY. What's Joshua's car seat doing out?

MADDY. I haven't made dinner. We've nothing in. We went to the shops but Joshua wouldn't wear the reins so we came back.

I know you don't like the reins but you're not with him all day. What did you have for lunch?

Stop looking at the car seat.

Take your jacket off at least. You look… all layered up with your jacket on.

Why don't men know when they're too hot?

RORY. Maddy…

MADDY. Don't. I don't want to tell you yet.

I did something. And once I've told you, I won't ever be able to untell it. And I can't decide. Because if I don't tell, you won't necessarily ever know and then we can just… be. Because if I do tell, then I'm not sure we can… just be… I think it might change a lot of things. Because Joshua. Joshua doesn't know what's normal and what isn't. So, he won't. I mean, he won't realise for years. If he remembers. But you. Do you want me to tell you? Or shall we just leave it? If it comes up we'll both know it's a problem and if not, we can, you know, just pretend.

Are you hungry? I should be hungry but… You look so serious. Stop looking so. Stop looking. Stop.

RORY. Maddy.

MADDY. See this mark on my arm. Here. I can't have been much older than Joshua. Mum and I baked a cake. I'd finished licking every spoon, bowl and spatula and she'd left the room for some reason. I wanted to see if the cake was ready so I opened the oven and reached in to touch the top of the cake to see if it bounced just like Mum did. But I leant my arm against the oven and… I never did it again. Burns heal. Sometimes they leave a mark, sometimes they don't. But the lesson is learnt and…

RORY. What did you do?

MADDY. Don't be angry. You start out angry and… I can't tell you if you're angry. I'll make us some dinner. I think we

have an egg, some cheese. I could make us a carbonara.
If you're hungry. Are you hungry?

RORY *shakes his head.*

I just want to keep him safe.

You were so sorry the other day. Sorry that he'd got through
the gate, sorry you still hadn't put the lock on, sorry that you
were filling up the paddling pool so didn't have your eye on
him, sorry that you'd got him so excited about being able to
ride a bike that he wanted to go out with it on his own. But
the one thing you weren't sorry about was leaving him alone
with that guy who stinks of dope and is kipping on the sofa
of a woman who lives on our street. That's why – why I want
to keep Joshua close to me and never let him out of my sight.
You talk about 'trust your gut', well I grew Joshua in my gut
and unless he's close by, all I feel there is hollow.

But I know, in my head, I know that's not right. I can't be
with him every minute of the day. I have to let him spend
time with you, with your mum. For him and for you. But that
leaves me with something of a predicament, you see. How
can I keep him safe when I'm not there if the people who
look after him are blind to the bad in people? So I made a
decision when I carried him to his bed that day that I would
have to find a way to teach him about the bad people. But
that's the thing about parenting, isn't it? You know there's
lessons you need to teach them but you don't know when is
the right time and then BANG, suddenly the opportunity
arises and you think, now. This is my chance, he's listening
now. Don't waste this opportunity to teach the lesson or
you'll regret it. And that happened to us today.

There was this article in the magazine from your Sunday
papers about sex tourism. There was a picture of Paul Gadd
all kitted out as Gary Glitter from our childhood. Joshua
peeped over my shoulder. 'Who's that, Mummy?' And I
covered the picture. Covered Gary Glitter's evil fucking face
so he couldn't hurt my boy and then I thought, don't do that.
Teach him. Keep him safe. So I uncovered it and Joshua

thought it was a game and said 'Peekaboo funny man.' And I stayed really calm and I said, 'That's not a funny man, Joshua. That man is evil. That man did bad things to little girls. If you ever see a man like that, you run away.' And then I thought that's the wrong lesson. Joshua's safe from Paul Gadd. He's never been into little boys, has he? I've never heard anything about him abusing little boys.

So while Joshua was having a nap – he was tired today. I went online and I found a site about paedophiles. With their pictures. Sometimes with their addresses too. It's a good website. Lots of details about their crimes so you know who's raped little boys and who's raped little girls and who's raped both. So when Joshua woke up, I said, 'Let's play a game.' I'm going to show you some pictures of bad men and you can remember their faces and make sure you never go near anybody like that.' And he thought that sounded fun. But I got it wrong. Because I should never have said it was a game. Because it's not is it? And he was giggling and saying things like. 'Hello, Mr Serious Face.' And I knew it wasn't working so then I thought, he needs to associate these faces with pain. You know, sort of Pavlov's dogs. So I… well, I got him to look really hard at the faces and then I pinched him. Hard, like this. But he didn't like that. Obviously. And he started getting upset and not looking at the faces. And it wasn't working so I brought in his car seat and I strapped him in and I held his head straight so he had to look and then I thought if we're doing this properly, pinching doesn't really cut it does it? So I lit a match and I held it to his hand while he looked at the faces. And he was squirming and crying and I was crying too, of course. But when he had looked at all the faces, I put ice on his hand and bandaged it and hugged him while he watched Fireman Sam and he cheered up really quickly. I really think it's okay. I think he learnt the lesson and is safer than ever now. I don't think he'll even remember how upset he was in the morning but if he ever sees a face like those I showed him, I think he'll be cautious without even realising why. So I think it was okay, really. In the end. You're not saying anything. Why aren't you saying anything?

RORY *walks over to the phone. Makes a call.*

What are you doing? Who are you phoning?

RORY (*on the phone*). Hi, Mum, it's me. Yes. Look, I need you to come over and collect Joshua for the night. Yes. Now. No. No. Please don't ask me any questions. Okay. Okay. Thank you.

RORY *puts down the receiver. A long silence.*

I want you to go to our room and stay there until Mum has collected Joshua. You are not to come out, even if he calls for you. Not even to say goodbye. Do you understand? Do. You. Understand?

MADDY. Yes.

RORY. Good.

Tomorrow we get you help.

A Rehabilitation Clinic

MADDY *wearing jogging trousers and top sits opposite* RORY. *They sit looking at each other for a while until…*

RORY. You've lost weight.

MADDY. You haven't.

RORY. Mum's cooking.

A silence.

How are you?

MADDY. I've been better.

RORY. Is it helping?

MADDY. If I say yes, can I come home?

RORY. –

MADDY. Five weeks. Five weeks and not a visit, not a phone call.

RORY. I couldn't. I've been so angry with you.

MADDY. Five weeks without seeing or speaking to Joshua.

RORY. You hurt him.

A silence.

MADDY. So why are you here now?

RORY. I don't want to be. I want to be anywhere but here.

MADDY. That makes two of us.

RORY. I wish I could hate you.

MADDY *takes a drink of water.*

MADDY. Want some?

RORY. Yes please.

MADDY *pours him a glass of water from the jug...*

MADDY (*in an uncanny impression of* MORVEN). Shall I be mother?

RORY. Don't take the piss out of her.

MADDY. Just a joke.

She drinks.

How's his hand?

RORY. Fine. It doesn't even look red any more.

MADDY (*through tears*). Good. Is he okay?

RORY. Who knows? He seems fine. He misses you.

MADDY. I miss him.

RORY. Has it been useful at all? Being here. The counselling?

MADDY *shrugs.*

Has talking helped? Has it changed the way you see things? The way you started to see the world?

MADDY. What do you want me to say?

RORY. What do I want you to say? What do I want you to say?
I'll tell you. I want you to say, I was wrong, I made a
mistake. I want you to say, I was ill and what I did to Joshua
was horrific. I see that now. I want you to say I'm well now,
completely and totally well, I am cured, one hundred per
cent, you can trust me, you can let me back into your lives
because I will never ever hurt either of you again. Because
that's what I want to do, Maddy. I want to bring you home.
Because I miss... the smell of you, your body next to mine,
the way you tug my hair when we kiss. And because Joshua
needs his mummy. And because, before all this, you were a
really brilliant mummy. It made me fall in love with you
twice over watching the way you were with that boy. All
through the pregnancy and in labour you were, you were
heroic. And the feeding when he couldn't get the latch and
you were red raw and you were so determined to make it
work and you sat there day after day, in pain from the
stitches where you'd torn, lifting him to your breast for
another agonising feed and you never once seemed to resent
him for all that pain. And when his little tummy hurt with
colic and he would scream all day long and I'd come home
and you'd be dancing with him, you'd have been dancing for
hours because that was the only thing that kept him happy.
And you were so tired but he would wake up two or three
times during the night and you were so gentle with him –
I used to hear you humming to him through the haze of my
disturbed sleep and I couldn't have loved you any more. And
the hours you've read to him, drawn with him, pushed him
on the swing, dawdled with him on the way home as he
brings you another hundred sticks and stones and you react
to each one like it's the best gift you have ever received.
And yes you were uptight about what he ate and watched
and bedtime and managing routines and that wasn't the way
I was raised but I even loved you for that because
everything, everything was for love of him. And I think
about the fact he nearly got run over when I was looking
after him and I know how awful I felt and I learnt from it but
it doesn't mean that I'm not allowed to be parent any more.

And that's what I want what you did to him to be – a horrible
accident. Because then I could hug you and say – I know,
I know you made a mistake but accidents happen and I know
you'd never ever hurt our boy.

The Supermarket Café

MADDY *stands with shopping bags.* MORVEN *enters with
a tray with a pot of tea for two.*

MADDY. This feels like a test.

MORVEN. Don't be ridiculous. It's tea and a bun.

MADDY. You want to see if it will bother me. To see if I'm well.

MORVEN. Are you well?

MADDY. I think so. Yes.

MORVEN. Good, no need for this place to bother you then.
Sit down.

MADDY. Do you think I'm well? You asked me. What do you
think?

MORVEN. I'm not a doctor.

MADDY. That's not an answer.

MORVEN. I just mean that any answer I give will be based on
instinct. That's all I'm saying.

MADDY. What does your gut tell you then?

MORVEN *takes a minute to think about her answer to this.*

MORVEN. That you are and always have been a lovely girl.

MADDY *is deeply touched by this. She sits.*

MADDY. Thank you.

MORVEN. What for?

MADDY. All of it. You've fed me up, kept things running smoothly and given me space when I've needed it. You've been a mother to all three of us.

MORVEN. It's what I do best.

MADDY. I don't know how we'll cope without you.

MORVEN. You won't have to.

MADDY. I just mean... when you move out.

MORVEN. Don't be silly. I'm not going anywhere.

MADDY. Do you not think it might be time? Soon.

MORVEN. No.

MADDY. Why not?

MORVEN *takes a moment to think about that and then very direct...*

MORVEN. I don't trust you yet. I don't trust you alone with Joshua.

MADDY. That's exactly how I felt about you.

MORVEN. They're not comparable. I didn't hurt Joshua.

MADDY. We'll never know though, will we? We'll never know if he was more scarred by what you did than...

MORVEN. Than what you did? Burning his hand?

MADDY. It was horrific. It doesn't matter that I did it out of love, I was in a very dangerous and dark place and I will wish it undone every single minute of my life.

MORVEN. But you can't undo it. Your name is on the Child Protection Register. There's a team of professionals who have decided that Joshua is only safe to stay at home because Rory and I are co-parenting. So let's have no more talk about me moving out. That's for me to decide and Rory. Not for you. Now then. Shall I be mother?

MORVEN *picks up the teapot and starts to pour.* MADDY *pulls the mug away. Tea spills everywhere.*

Maddy! What a mess. What did you do that for?

MADDY. I do get a say actually. The social worker has been in touch. It's been agreed that I pose no future risk to Joshua. The state says I'm allowed to be Joshy's mummy again. So I do get a say now, Morven.

MORVEN. Does Rory know?

MADDY. Of course he does.

RORY *not telling* MORVEN *is a betrayal and* MADDY *knows it.*

Let me be Joshua's mummy. You can see him all you like. Be his granny.

But let me be his mummy again. Please.

MORVEN. No.

MADDY. You have to.

MORVEN. Why's that?

MADDY. Because I'm pregnant.

MORVEN. –

MADDY. A new baby is coming into this world and I'll be its mummy, not you. So it's time, don't you think? It's time for you to move out and let me and Rory and Joshua be a family again.

MADDY *picks up the pot and pours herself and* MORVEN *a cup of tea.*

Joshua's Nursery

MADDY *has just collected Joshua from nursery. He is playing with his friend in the yard outside, just out of sight.* THE STRANGER *approaches her.*

MADDY (*to offstage Joshua*). Don't throw them, Joshy. No, you'll hurt Jamie if you throw that at him. You can play with them but don't throw, okay?

THE STRANGER NURSERY DAD. Can't drag either of them away from the stones.

MADDY. No.

THE STRANGER NURSERY DAD. Jamie's been asking and asking if he can have Joshua round to play.

MADDY. Awww, Joshua's desperate to see Jamie's giant dinosaur.

THE STRANGER NURSERY DAD. He could come to ours if he liked? Have some lunch.

MADDY. Do you mean on his own?

THE STRANGER NURSERY DAD. Well, yeah. So they can play. I presume you're local?

MADDY. Yes. Just round the corner. Today?

THE STRANGER NURSERY DAD. If it suits. They're having a ball just now, seems a shame to break up the bromance.

MADDY. Why doesn't Jamie come to us for a playdate?

THE STRANGER NURSERY DAD. And miss the giant dinosaur?

MADDY. Right. Yes. Um, okay. Yeah.

My husband is actually just speaking to the nursery manager to go through some stuff. He'll be out any minute. Do you mind if we wait for him? See what he says.

THE STRANGER NURSERY DAD. I think I've met your husband and Joshy's 'granny', is it?

MADDY. Yeah. So you're local too are you?

THE STRANGER NURSERY DAD. We're on Kelvindale Road. Number Five.

MADDY. We're Sixty-five!

THE STRANGER NURSERY DAD. We're neighbours then.

MADDY. Yes. How funny.

An awkward pause.

THE STRANGER NURSERY DAD. Look, if you'd rather arrange something for another day…? I just thought it would make Jamie's week if –

MADDY. No, that's… It would be a shame for them to miss out. So, um, yeah. I'm sure Rory will say yes. Joshua would love that.

THE STRANGER NURSERY DAD. Okay then. Great.

MADDY. I'd better take your number, then I can text you mine.

THE STRANGER NURSERY DAD. Of course. I'm 07811548440.

RORY *enters.*

MADDY. Rory! Jamie's dad is going to take Joshua for a little playdate. Is that okay?

RORY. Of course. What a lovely idea. (*To* THE STRANGER NURSERY DAD.) Hi again. How are your ears after all that shouting our boys were doing last week?

THE STRANGER NURSERY DAD. Pardon?

RORY. I said, how are your… (*Realises it was a joke.*) You're joking. Good one.

MADDY. They live at number Five.

RORY. Great. I'm heading back to work but maybe Maddy could pick Joshua up in what? A couple of hours? That sound good?

THE STRANGER NURSERY DAD. Suits me.

(*To* MADDY.) Is that okay?

MADDY. Yes. That's fine. Joshua. Joshua. How do you fancy going to Jamie's house for a wee play?

Thought you'd like that. Give Mummy a big hug then.

JOSHUA *walks on stage. He's a tiny wee thing, clutching a handful of stones, arms out to hug his mummy.* MADDY *holds him in a long hug, kisses him and composes herself to let him go.*

THE STRANGER NURSERY DAD. Come on then, Joshua. Help me prise Jamie away from those stones so we can get home and see his giant dinosaur.

RORY. Have fun, Joshua.

They start to leave.

MADDY. Wait!

You'd better take his coat.

She gives THE STRANGER NURSERY DAD JOSHUA*'s coat.*

THE STRANGER NURSERY DAD. See you in a couple of hours.

They watch them leave, JOSHUA*'s little hand in the hand of* THE STRANGER.

MADDY. That's okay then, isn't it? That was the right thing to do?

RORY. You saw Joshua's face – he was over the moon.

MADDY. Yes but I mean... he'll be safe there?

RORY. Of course.

A seed of doubt. Can we ever say that with total confidence?

Of course he will.

Neither are entirely convinced. They both stand watching after their little boy, anxiety rising. Hoping for the best.

Blackout.

A Nick Hern Book

Gut first published as a paperback original in Great Britain in 2018 by Nick Hern Books Limited, The Glasshouse, 49a Goldhawk Road, London W12 8QP, in association with the Traverse Theatre, Edinburgh

Gut copyright © 2018 Frances Poet

Frances Poet has asserted her right to be identified as the author of this work

Cover design by Michael Cranston

Designed and typeset by Nick Hern Books, London
Printed in the UK by Mimeo Ltd, Huntingdon, Cambridgeshire PE29 6XX

A CIP catalogue record for this book is available from the British Library

ISBN 978 1 84842 716 7

www.nickhernbooks.co.uk

facebook.com/nickhernbooks

twitter.com/nickhernbooks